DT
767
I5

PROPERTY OF

DT 767 I5
California Maritime Academy Library (CSU)

3 0060 00028514 6

D0883356

DT
767
I5

Maritime South Africa:
a pictorial history

To Margaret, Graeme and Andrew
BRIAN INGPEN

To Emmie, Rainer and Gabriela
ROBERT PABST

PROPERTY OF
CALIFORNIA MARITIME ACADEMY
LIBRARY

28514

Maritime South Africa:
a pictorial history

Brian Ingpen and
Robert Pabst

JANE'S

First published in the United Kingdom in
1985 by Jane's Publishing Company Ltd
238 City Road
London EC1V 2PU

Text © B.D. Ingpen and R.F.W. Pabst 1984
All rights reserved. No part of this publication
may be reproduced, stored in a retrieval system,
or transmitted in any form or by any means,
electronic, mechanical, photocopying, recording
or otherwise, without the prior written
permission of the copyright owners.

First published 1985

Distributed in the Philippines and the
USA and its dependencies by
Jane's Publishing Inc
135 West 50th Street
New York NY 10020

ISBN 0 7106 0351 7

PRELIMINARY-PAGE PHOTOGRAPHS
Page 1: Unicorn Lines' multi-purpose vessel
Gamtoos.
Page 2: At sea aboard the Unicorn coaster *Kowie.*
Page 3: A painting by Peter Bilas of the
Dromedaris, the vessel in which Jan van
Riebeeck sailed to the Cape in 1652.
Page 4: An officer on watch aboard the *Kowie.*
Pages 4 and 5: With coal-burning tugs in
attendance, the *Windsor Castle* leaves Table Bay
harbour.
Pages 6 and 7: Safmarine's container ship *S.A.
Langeberg.*

Contents

Acknowledgements 6
Foreword 7

1. Introduction 8
2. Harbours 18
3. The Naval Tradition 44
4. Passenger Services 72
5. The Cargo Trade 98
6. Suez Closures 130
7. Maritime Casualties 138
8. Maritime Miscellany 154

Bibliography 174
Photographic Credits 174
Index 175

SOUTHERN AFRICA: PRESENT AND FORMER PORTS, AND MAIN INLAND CENTRES

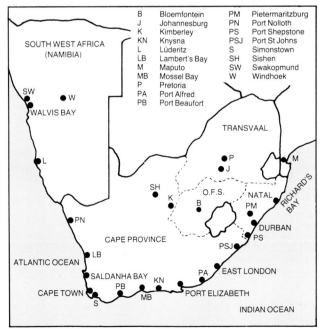

B	Bloemfontein	PM	Pietermaritzburg
J	Johannesburg	PN	Port Nolloth
K	Kimberley	PS	Port Shepstone
KN	Knysna	PSJ	Port St Johns
L	Lüderitz	S	Simonstown
LB	Lambert's Bay	SH	Sishen
M	Maputo	SW	Swakopmund
MB	Mossel Bay	W	Windhoek
P	Pretoria		
PA	Port Alfred		
PB	Port Beaufort		

Acknowledgements

Although the story of maritime South Africa is well documented in the collections of various museums, libraries, archives, shipping companies, societies, and private individuals, it is obviously not possible for everyone interested in shipping and maritime history to gain access to all these sources. Our book makes a selection of such material more readily available, and we thereby hope not only to provide satisfaction for enthusiasts but also to stimulate a wider interest in a fascinating aspect of South Africa's history.

We are extremely grateful to the Ship Society of South Africa for placing at our disposal the unique photographic collection of the late Martin Leendertz, and to the staff of the following institutions for being so patient and helpful: the South African Library, the South African National Museum for Military History, the Local History Museum, Durban, the Cape Archives, the Natal Archival Depot, the State Archives, Windhoek, the Simonstown Museum and the Bredasdorp Museum.

Detailed photographic credits can be found at the end of the book, but the following individuals deserve special mention for their willingness to supply material: (in alphabetical order) Dr Errol Cornish; Clyde Davidson; Raymond Hancock; Captain C.J. Harris; H.E. Healing; Eric Hoskings; Werner Kaufmann; Mrs M. Parkes (Knysna); Mrs M. Sands and Mrs M. Thomson (Swellendam); Professor Les Underhill; the Reverend Don Williams.

Particular thanks are due to Peter Bilas for making several of his superb maritime paintings available for reproduction.

The management and staff of Safmarine, Unicorn Lines and Irvin & Johnson were most generous in their offers of photographic material, while Commanders Stephen, Bisset and Visser of the South African Navy spared no effort to help and advise.

We are grateful to Peter Borchert and Douglas van der Horst of Struik for their role in producing the book, and to the designer, Neville Poulter, for his sympathetic response to the material.

Finally we must thank our respective wives, Margaret and Emmie, for their constant support and encouragement, even in the most trying circumstances.

Brian Ingpen
Robert Pabst

Foreword

This is a magnificent pictorial record of our maritime history. The subject is well researched, the breadth of coverage impressive and the text very readable.

It is strange that the descendants of European settlers who came over the water to a sub-continent where two great oceans divide have done so little to preserve their maritime heritage. We who are involved in shipping are often surprised at the lack of real knowledge of an industry which is so vital to our nation's well-being. This book with its wealth of information will therefore fulfil a real need. It is not only for the enthusiast but also for the uninitiated and indeed the scholar.

Included are the great shipping enterprises and the fine ships which provided our passenger services and economic lifeline for so long. The country's maritime infrastructure is well documented – from the small, romantic and almost forgotten ports, to the magnificent modern harbours of today.

The authors also cover our proud naval record and the many facets of our comparatively young merchant marine. Having devoted nearly a lifetime to the merchant marine, I am impressed by the authors' sympathetic understanding of our aspirations and problems. The men who sail our ships under the umbrella of the Senior Service will appreciate this record of their achievements. Today our merchant ships proudly show the South African flag in most of the world's great ports. Our vital coastal, short-sea and fishing industries complete a fascinating story.

I must congratulate the authors on a worthwhile task well done. It has been a rare privilege and pleasure for me to write this foreword to their splendid effort.

M. De W. Marsh
Executive Chairman
South African Marine Corporation Limited

SOUTH AFRICA'S development is closely linked to the sea, and its continued prosperity depends largely on its maritime infrastructure. Along its coast is one of the world's major trade routes, a seaway which is of considerable strategic importance because it remains the only viable alternative to the Suez Canal for ships travelling between Europe and the East.

The story of maritime South Africa in fact begins with the attempts by early mariners from Europe to discover this sea route. Although there are some references in ancient literature which suggest that Phoenician sailors may have circumnavigated Africa in about 600 B.C., the first reliable documents in South African maritime history are the accounts of the Portuguese voyages of exploration in the fifteenth century. The first of these expeditions to reach the southern part of Africa was led by Bartholomew Diaz, who landed at various places along the coast, including present-day Lüderitz and Mossel Bay, in 1487, but who was forced by his crew to curtail the search for a sea passage to the East. Although Diaz failed to complete the mission, his exploration of a large part of the route made it possible for his countryman, Vasco da Gama, to reach India a decade later.

Other pioneering navigators, including Sir Francis Drake, also came this way, and contributed to the increasing recognition of the Cape route as an important seaway. During the sixteenth and seventeenth centuries there was a steady increase in the numbers of Portuguese, British and Dutch ships trading along this route. As a result of clashes with the indigenous peoples at Table Bay, Mossel Bay and elsewhere, the Portuguese preferred Delagoa Bay (Maputo) as a port of call. However, the

CHAPTER
INTRODUCTION
I

British and Dutch continued to use Table Bay and occasionally also called at other anchorages along the South African coast ■

1 The Cape Peninsula (seen here from the west) was for many centuries the focal point of maritime activity along the coast of Southern Africa.

2 A painting by Peter Bilas of the phantom ship *Flying Dutchman*. According to legend this vessel, as a result of her captain's blasphemous defiance of God, was condemned to struggle eternally against wind and current in an attempt to round the Cape of Good Hope. Many sailors claim to have sighted the vessel, including the future King George V when he was a midshipman aboard HMS *Bachante*.

1

IN THIS AGE of air-conditioned cruise liners, supertankers, and nuclear-powered ships, it is hard to believe that the early sailing vessels which passed our shores were barely the size of modern fishing craft. They had to be sufficiently provisioned to spend months, even years, at sea, and their crews frequently had to carry out makeshift repairs or sometimes complete overhauls at remote anchorages using local timber. Every voyage was an epic. Some expeditions went according to plan, while others were dogged by misfortune. Many ships ran foul of the treacherous shoals, in-shore currents or fog along our coast-line, and were dashed to pieces, their crews enduring great suffering as they clung to flotsam until their strength gave in.

The Dutch East India Company recognized the need to replenish their ships and rest the crews, and consequently Jan van Riebeeck and his party were sent to the Cape in 1652 to establish a refreshment station halfway between Europe and the East. Thus the first passengers were landed, and point-to-point shipping services to South Africa began. The Cape settlement had to cater annually for the vast number of meals required by seamen on the outward or homeward fleets, and this marked the beginning of organized ship chandling in South Africa.

Only after the second British occupation of the Cape in 1806 did local shipping and commerce advance significantly. The need to provide supplies for the Cape garrison and the soldiers on St Helena who guarded Napoleon from 1815 to 1821 stimulated the economy of the colony, while the arrival of settlers, particularly those of 1820, led to a further increase in shipping services, not only between Britain and Southern Africa but also along the coast. The flourishing colony of Natal also altered the shipping scene, direct sailings being introduced between England and Port Natal (Durban) in the 1850s ■

1 Early morning at Cape Recife, the south-western point of Algoa Bay. The vessels carrying the 1820 Settlers sailed around this headland and anchored in the bay off present-day Port Elizabeth.
2 A Bucknall steamer at East London, c. 1900.
3 Durban's Bluff, a landmark familiar to sailors since the earliest times. Vasco da Gama is thought to have anchored off the Bluff in 1497 to catch fish.

2

3

WITH REGARD to maritime technology, perhaps the most significant advance of the time occurred in 1825, when the *Enterprise,* the first steamship to call here, put into Table Bay; thereafter sail slowly but surely gave way to steam.

Foreign and local events continued to influence shipping trends. During the Australian gold rush in the mid-nineteenth century, hundreds of ships called at the Cape. Although the opening of the Suez Canal in 1869 led to a decline in transit traffic, compensation came when diamonds were discovered in South Africa. Local waterfronts were soon crowded with hopefuls, the ships which had brought them causing congestion at port anchorages. About eighteen years later the Transvaal gold discoveries brought further armadas, which forced realistic harbour development projects to commence because the volume of passengers, equipment and stores for the mines had become too great for the hazardous landing arrangements in the roadsteads.

As described in Chapter Three, more chaos followed at the turn of the century, when military transports brought troops and supplies to South Africa during the Anglo-Boer War. This situation was repeated during the First and Second World Wars, the Cape route becoming a focal point for troopships and convoys travelling between the Indian and Atlantic Oceans.

To protect the Cape and shipping from attack, the Royal Navy had located a permanent base in South Africa in the nineteenth century. The naval tradition that was established here provided the foundation for the South African Navy, whose defensive capabilities have increased remarkably in the last two decades. South Africans in fast strike craft and submarines now guard our longest border.

Passenger services to South Africa developed throughout the nineteenth century and reached their peak in the first half of this century, when Union-Castle mailships, other British liners, and vessels flying the Dutch, German, Italian and Portuguese flags became familiar sights in our harbours. Increased operating costs and the advent of containerization led to the disappearance of regular passenger liners in the 1960s and 1970s ■

1 In modern naval architecture right-angles and welding are used, as opposed to curves and rivets. Today a great deal of attention is given to all aspects of safety at sea, and a simple yet important advance in this area is the increasing practice nowadays of painting lifeboats orange instead of the customary white, thus making air-sea searches for survivors of maritime casualties much easier.
2 Leaving Cape Town after her call during a training cruise is the barque *Grossherzogin Elizabeth.*
3 Compare the functional stern of this ro-ro vessel, the *Elgaren,* with the more graceful lines of the *Grossherzogin Elizabeth.*

1936. Subsequently the *Carnarvon Castle,* the *Edinburgh Castle* and the *Windsor Castle* clipped the time even further, and towards the end of the mailship era a normal passage took 11½ days (though in the 1970s the ageing *Edinburgh Castle* and *S.A. Oranje* found the schedule heavy going).

However, the record for the passage was not set by a Union-Castle liner. During the Second World War the *Queen Mary* apparently did the run in 9½ days!

This magnificent study of the *Athlone Castle* was taken by Eric Hoskings from the southbound *Capetown Castle* in 1959. Northbound and southbound mailships passed at the Canary Islands, in Cape Town and in Port Elizabeth, but it was the ceremonial passing at sea that was remembered so well, for the liners closed each other at 21 knots.

4 The triple-screw Dutch liner *Ruys* on her last voyage from Durban. Those who sailed in her or her sister ships, the *Boissevain* and the *Tegelberg,* still talk of the comfort aboard these vessels. But, as described in Chapter Four, these and all the passenger ships on the South African trade had to make way for cargo liners when the passenger trade declined.

1 In the days of sail, wind-jammers and men-of-war usually had a figurehead on the stem, just below the bowsprit. The modern vessels of the Christensen Canadian African Line still carry a figurehead (shown here), which depicts the Scandinavian god Thor, whose name prefixes the names of all the ships owned by this company.
2 An interesting study of the seaman's constant battle against the corrosion of steel.
3 The Union-Castle Line (formed by the merger of two rival lines, the Union Line and the Castle Line, in 1900) held the contract to carry mail between England and South Africa. This contract required the holder to maintain such a punctual schedule that minutes were of vital importance. The *Athlone Castle* (shown here) was built in Belfast yards in 1934/5 and was one of the vessels which Union-Castle Line put into service for the revised mail contract requiring a 14-day passage between Southampton and Cape Town instead of the nearly 17-day schedule previously allowed. Back in 1893 the *Scot* had completed the passage in 14 days, 9 hours, a record which stood until the *Stirling Castle* did the voyage in 13 days, 9 hours in

3

4

1

2

UNTIL THE Second World
War the South African
merchant navy was
limited to tiny coasters on the
local seaboard and to a few deep-
sea ships trading mainly to
Australia to load railway
sleepers. After the war the
situation changed greatly, and
today a large number of highly
sophisticated South African
vessels sail to tight schedules on
both the foreign and local trades.
The fleets of the two South
African shipping companies,
Safmarine and Unicorn Lines,
can compare and compete
favourably with other
international concerns.
    Cargo handling has been
revolutionized in the era of the
container vessel and the
supertanker: functional ships
with functional shapes now ply

heavily rationalized trades. In the process, some of the funnel colours of former years have disappeared as a result of intricate financial transactions or bankruptcy. Sentiment has played little part in the search for profits in the shipping world.

The fortunes of some early harbours have also fluctuated, and there are places along our coastline where formerly bustling jetties lie quiet, forgotten and decaying. Elsewhere harbour expansion has been extensive and rapid; modern technology is apparent at every turn, and our major ports reflect the remarkable economic development that has taken place in South Africa in the relatively short period since the mineral discoveries of the nineteenth century ∎

1 Safmarine's *S.A. Vergelegen* arrives at the Table Bay pilot station. She and four similar ships, as well as three heavy-lift vessels, entered service to replace older tonnage in the late 1960s. With the introduction of containerization on all Safmarine's trade routes, most of these vessels have themselves been replaced by large container ships.
2 Since the Second World War the ship repair industry has expanded, largely because of the reputation which the industry acquired during the war and the subsequent closures of the Suez Canal in 1956 and 1967. Because of the size of vessels and the pressure on the dry-docking facilities, new techniques for underwater repairs and maintenance have been developed. Here propeller maintenance work is being done.
3 The berthing launch takes the head-ropes from the German vessel *Weserland.* This ship and her sisters, the *Ostfriesland* and the *Hannoverland,* were on charter to Safmarine in the 1970s.

THE CONSTRUCTION OF harbours in South Africa arose initially from the need to provide ships with shelter and thus avoid loss of life, vessels and cargo. Further harbour development was linked to the discovery of minerals in the interior and the need to cater for the unprecedented volume of maritime traffic that followed these discoveries. The establishment of railway links between the ports and the mining areas, and the growth of local industry, led to the additional expansion of harbours and the general improvement of port facilities.

Today, with container terminals at Durban, Port Elizabeth and Cape Town, bulk handling facilities for minerals and agricultural products, pre-cooling stores and oil terminals, South Africa's harbours are able to handle a great volume and variety of freight. The recent commissioning of Richard's Bay and Saldanha Bay for the bulk

CHAPTER II

HARBOURS

export of coal and iron ore respectively, has once again underlined the country's dependence on sea-borne trade for its economic survival.

But some formerly thriving harbours, such as Port Alfred, Knysna and Port St Johns, are no longer in use; the once bustling waterfronts now lie quiet or are used for other purposes – testimony to frequent strandings, or to the development of road and rail transport, or simply to the growth of bigger and better harbours elsewhere ■

1 In August 1852 the coaster *Sir Robert Peel* became the first steamship to cross the bar at Durban. She belonged to the General Screw Steam Ship Company and was on the coastal trade for about two years.
2 The *S.A. Oranje* entering Durban harbour at first light. This photograph was taken from the bridge when she called at Durban for the last time.

DURING THE LAST century the rush for 'white gold' (guano) on the islands off the South West African coast, the existence of rich fishing grounds along that coast and the growth of trade in the interior, led to the establishment of three ports in the Namib Desert: Swakopmund in the north served the central and northern part of German-controlled South West Africa; Walvis Bay, immediately to the south, was a British possession (annexed in 1878 partly to facilitate the policing of the guano trade); and Lüderitzbucht (later Lüderitz), which lay in the bay named Angra Pequena by the early Portuguese navigators. At all three ports larger ships anchored off-shore and were served by lighters. This was often a hazardous operation because of the fickleness of the weather, particularly at Lüderitz.

After the surrender of South West Africa to South African forces in 1915, Swakopmund ceased to be a port and Walvis Bay started to expand. Its first commercial wharf was opened in 1927 and today it is the premier port in the region. Its fishing industry, the mineral exploitation in its hinterland, as well as the agricultural and industrial activities around Windhoek, provide it with a reasonable amount of cargo.

And what of Lüderitz, so prominent in the days of German South West Africa, when the white gold of the islands and the diamonds of the desert made this tiny port a place of great activity? The fortune seekers came and many towns grew, but then diamond prospecting became more controlled and people left. Lüderitz is now a much depleted place, sustained by the fishing industry, though even this has declined. The only vessels that call there now are fishing craft and the monthly coaster ■

1 A fine sailing ship at Walvis Bay's wooden jetty. Concrete structures with modern equipment are found here now, and the harbour is relatively busy with the export of mineral concentrates and fish products. A weekly service, operated by container ships, provides a feeder for the international container network.
2 The Swakopmund pier, built in 1905, was a landing stage rather than a place for larger vessels to berth. An iron jetty was started in 1911 but was incomplete when South West Africa was captured from Germany in 1915.
3 Seen off Lüderitz between the wars is the *Wangoni,* one of Deutsche Ost-Afrika Linie's round-Africa vessels. She was taken over by the Russians at the end of the Second World War and sailed under their flag for about twenty years. (Judging by the flag at the stern, this photograph was taken before 1933; thereafter she would have flown the Swastika flag.)

1 An aerial view of Lambert's Bay, a fishing port on the West Coast. Parallel to the coast at this point is the railway line which was specially constructed for transporting iron ore from Sishen in the northern Cape to Saldanha.

2 Another fishing harbour on the West Coast is Port Nolloth, just south of the Orange River mouth. A coaster service links this port to Cape Town, from where supplies are brought for the fishing industry and for the open-cast diamond mines at Alexander Bay, Oranjemund and Kleinsee. Some supplies for the Namaqualand copper mines also arrive via this service. From 1876 to 1944 a narrow-gauge railway brought copper from Okiep to Port Nolloth for export, mainly to Britain.

3 Unicorn Lines' coaster *Swazi* alongside the commercial wharf at Port Nolloth in 1973. Because of a narrow channel, a shallow reef and a confined turning area, only small vessels with a shallow draught can enter the harbour. The *Swazi* went aground there in 1972 but was refloated. She has been succeeded by the

Oranjemund, which calls there every ten days and occasionally also visits Lüderitz and Lambert's Bay.

4 The ore loaders at Saldanha, part of the huge scheme which came into operation in 1976 and involved the construction of a breakwater, an ore stacking area, a railway network, and port control buildings. At full capacity some 15 million tons of iron ore are exported per annum, mainly to Japan and Western Europe. Saldanha Bay is perhaps the best natural harbour on the South African coast and it is conceivable that it would have been used to a far greater extent by early mariners had it not been for an insufficient supply of fresh water.

5 The Saldanha jetty from the ore-stacking control tower.

6 Simon's Bay in October 1899. The ships on the slipway in the foreground are HMS *Thrush* (right) and HM Torpedo Boats 6 and 15 (left). In the bay are, from left to right, HM Survey Ship *Rambler,* HMS *Doris,* HMS *Powerful,* HMS *Monarch* and HMS *Penelope.* The last-mentioned was used later to accommodate Boer prisoners of war.

7 The final stages in the construction of Simonstown harbour in 1908. The Selborne graving dock is just visible behind the row of buildings.

IN TABLE BAY a few attempts had been made to build jetties, even one where farmers were obliged to use their wagons to transport stone from the quarries on Signal Hill to the construction site near Mouille Point after they had taken their produce to market. But the frequency and ferocity of winter storms, and the increasing volume of cargo and number of passengers being landed, required something more substantial. An enclosed harbour, the Alfred Basin, was eventually completed in 1870, followed by the Victoria Basin before the end of the century. The most important developments since then have been the construction of the Duncan Dock and the Ben Schoeman Container Basin ■

1 A painting by Thomas Bowler which depicts the ceremony in 1860 at which Prince Alfred tipped a load of stones into Table Bay to mark the official commencement of the building of the first enclosed basin in Southern Africa. Convicts from the notorious Breakwater Prison hewed the rock by hand. When completed in 1870, the Alfred Basin was too small, for in the interim the diamond riches of Kimberley had brought a rush of shipping to Table Bay.
2 The old port offices and port control centre (the clock tower)

stand on either side of the former harbour entrance.

3 The Alfred Basin is now used by trawlers (many of which are larger than some of the early liners) and by Cape snoekers.

4 The Alfred Basin during the last century. At least nine sailing vessels are berthed here and more are visible outside the harbour. Double-banking, as seen here, greatly inconvenienced cargo work.

3

4

millions of cubic metres of material were dredged up and used for the reclamation of what is now Cape Town's 'Foreshore' area.

Seen here in the Duncan Dock is the *Windsor Castle* in from Southampton. Beyond is the Ben Schoeman Container Basin, inaugurated by Safmarine's *S.A. Morgenster* in 1977.

5 The tugs *F.T. Bates* and *T.S. McEwen* attend the Farrell Line freighter *African Comet* in 1963 at B Berth, which is alongside one of Table Bay harbour's pre-cooling stores for the shipment of fruit and fish.

1 The Alfred Basin with one steamer alongside West Quay. At the turn of the century, sail was still dominant.

2 The Union-Castle liners *Goorkha* and *Dunvegan Castle* at the present Number 2 Jetty in the Victoria Basin, the first major extension to Table Bay harbour. Note the cabs and also the railway trucks loaded with coal, probably for ship's bunkers.

3 An Ellerman and Bucknall cargo liner at Number 2 Jetty in the late 1960s. This berth is used mainly by fishing craft, but coastal shipments of fish oil are also loaded here.

4 In response to industrial expansion, to the congestion experienced during the First World War and to the increasing size of the Union-Castle mailships, work began in the 1930s on additional berths which now form part of the Duncan Dock, completed in 1945. During the building of the Duncan Dock,

3

4

5

1 Joseph Barry, one of the shipping pioneers of the Breede River, where Port Beaufort and the upstream jetty at Malgas were in operation from about 1850 to 1865. From here wool and wheat were shipped to Table Bay and occasionally to England.
2 The steamer *Kadie,* which was built in Britain for the Breede River-Cape Town trade. The vessel was lost on the bar at the river mouth in 1865, an incident which led to the closure of the river ports. In the mid-1930s there was a failed attempt to reopen the Breede River trade, this time using the former water-tanker *Chub* (see page 121).
3 Thesen's coaster *Agnar* and two whalers at the Knysna wharf. This port served the southern Cape, mainly from the middle of the last century until 1940, during which period timber was shipped to Cape Town and Port Elizabeth. The development of overland trade routes made Knysna redundant as a port.
4 HMSAS *Protea* leaving Knysna.
5 The shipment of aloes and

ostrich feathers, and the establishment of railway links to the interior, stimulated the development of Mossel Bay and required the construction of a breakwater and jetty in 1912. However, larger ships, including Union-Castle liners, still had to work cargo in the roadstead, a practice which has long since disappeared. Offshore gas discoveries and oil prospecting hold out some hope for the port, which is at present visited only by coasters and the occasional tanker.

6 The coaster *Clara* loading timber at Storms River mouth early this century.

1

2

3

ALTHOUGH a fort was built at Algoa Bay in 1799, the establishment of Port Elizabeth took place only when the British settlers arrived in 1820. As trade through the port increased, various attempts at jetty construction were made. However, the results of these attempts provided landing stages rather than berths for ocean-going ships, and the vessels anchored in the bay were still unprotected. The location in the area of two motor-car assembly plants in the 1920s, together with increasing wool exports, finally led to the building of an artificial basin, completed in 1938 ∎

1 The dawn arrival of a Safmarine container ship.
2 The Dom Pedro Jetty, completed in 1902, was used to load and discharge lighters until the sheltered deep-sea wharves came into use in 1938.
3 The Donkin Reserve overlooks Port Elizabeth harbour.
4 Sailing ships riding out a gale in Algoa Bay. Frequent strandings occurred here: in 1902 one of the 'great gales' caused the loss of nineteen ships in a single night.
5 The Norwegian cruise liner *Vistafjord* passes Port Elizabeth's container terminal.

4

5

AFTER 1820 A NUMBER OF river mouths and bays were explored to test their suitability as anchorages for the expanding frontier settlements of the eastern Cape. Port Alfred, originally Port Frances, at the mouth of the Kowie River, was envisaged as a major port for the area. Indeed, around 1840 a great deal of planning and money went into improvements to the river mouth and into the construction of wharfage. Local produce was exported from here to Table Bay and even to Britain. But competition from the expanding town of Port

Elizabeth, and frequent strandings on the notorious bar, led to the decline of the port and the eventual termination of trade in 1900 ■

1, 2 Two water-colours showing views of Port Alfred in its

heyday. The wharves and warehouses are put to other uses now.

3 The old customs house guards the entrance to the Kowie River.

4 Improvements under way in earlier times at Port Alfred. The old paddle-tug at the port ended her days on a sandbank.

5 During the frontier wars of the last century the mouth of the Great Fish River and other such bays were landing places for British troops and their equipment. The heavy surf and the exposure of these bays to gales precluded their commercial use.

THE FIRST RECORDED discovery of the Buffalo River by European settlers was made in the seventeenth century by a group of explorers sent out by Simon van der Stel, the Dutch governor of the Cape. Only during the frontier wars in the nineteenth century, however, did the mouth of the river assume any significance.

Trading increased in the area, particularly after the arrival of the German settlers in 1857, and harbour construction began in earnest in 1872. Thus South Africa's only river port, East London, was born.

Initially most ships anchored in the roadstead and were worked by lighter, passengers being landed or embarked by the 'basket-and-tug' method. But by 1924 even the Union-Castle liners were entering the port. To accommodate the bigger Union-Castle ships, the turning basin was enlarged twice ■

1 East London harbour in about 1898. Two of the port's earlier steam tugs are seen on the right.
2 East London's shifting

sandbanks, caused by a combination of river flow and tidal scour, have become notorious over the years. The propeller wash of ships, even in modern times, is likely to stir up the sand. The clanking of dredgers has therefore been part of the scene since 1886. The old bucket-dredgers are now making way for modern craft.

3 The Deutsche Ost-Afrika Linie vessel *Njassa* lies alongside the East Bank during the 1920s.

4 The Italian liner *Duilio* at East London sometime after 1933. This was the berth where, after the Second World War and until their rescheduling in the 1970s, the Union-Castle mailships docked every Monday and Friday.

THE NATURAL restrictions on the depth of water and the narrowness of the river mouth have limited the growth of East London harbour. It was overlooked in the planning for deep-sea container facilities but, oddly enough, has been used for the export of copper from Central Africa when access to the more natural outlets for the mineral has been blocked by various upheavals.

On the coast between East London and Durban are Port St Johns and Port Shepstone, both of which served a useful purpose

before the growth of more efficient road and rail transport made them obsolete ■

1 East London harbour in 1983.
2 The narrowness of the Buffalo River valley is obvious from this view looking upstream to the bridges. Until Port Elizabeth's harbour was built, East London was the country's major centre for the export of wool. The weekly mailship (and practically every other vessel in port during the wool season) used to take on hundreds of tons of wool, making the call most profitable.

Sometimes there was so much wool to load that the mailship left late and had to increase speed to keep to schedule.
3 Port St Johns, at the mouth of the Umzimvubu River. A Portuguese vessel, the *São João* (St John), was apparently stranded here in the sixteenth century. Coasters trading mainly out of Durban called here occasionally from 1847, but more regular services began in 1889. These small vessels crossed the bar in an unusual way. From a nearby hillside the pilot would decide where the channel lay at that time and would give directions to men who waded into the river mouth and marked the edge of the channel with flags.

Despite this procedure ships frequently came to grief. This problem, combined with improved road links, led to the closure of the port in 1946.
4 A similar but briefer story belongs to Port Shepstone on the Umzimkulu River. From 1880 small steamers proceeded up the river for about 13 kilometres to load sugar cane. But entering the river was also quite an event. One early photograph shows men (perhaps convicts from the local jail) using long poles to prevent a steamer from grounding at the breakwater. When the railway to Durban was completed in 1901, the sugar cane went by rail and the port closed. Seen in this photograph is the coaster *Somtseu*.

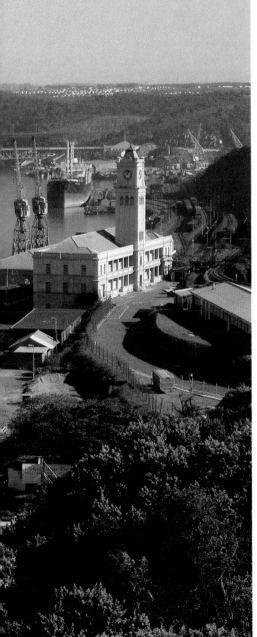

WHEN LIEUTENANTS Farewell and King forced their brig over the bar at Port Natal while on a trading expedition in 1823, they could not have imagined the vast development that would take place there. The sheltered and extensive Durban Bay has subsequently become Africa's busiest commercial harbour. Its initial growth was stimulated by the development of the Transvaal goldfields (from 1888), the railway link with Johannesburg (1895), and the Anglo-Boer War (1899-1902). The post-Union era has seen remarkable growth, attributable not only to industrial development in the interior, but also to Durban's own expanding industries. Today the harbour occupies a water area of 892 hectares, has over 15 kilometres of wharfage for commercial shipping, and handles more than 20 million tons of cargo annually (excluding petroleum products) ∎

1 Sailing ships at St Paul's Pier, Durban.
2 Timber (for building construction, railway sleepers and mine props) being unloaded from sailing ships at the Point (c. 1900).
3 A steamer and sailing ships in Durban Bay.
4 This photograph was perhaps taken at the time of the relief of Ladysmith during the Anglo-Boer War.
5 Indians aboard a steam launch and a lighter during the last century. It is not clear whether the photograph depicts dock labourers or the arrival of Indians in Durban for employment on the sugar plantations.
6 Ox wagons provided early links with the port's hinterland. They would trundle over the cobbles on their way to the Natal interior or even to the Transvaal, carrying all kinds of cargoes, from spades, tents and clothing to weapons, provisions and timber.

3

4

5

6

1 Ships triple-banked in Durban Bay because of a shortage of berths (*c.* 1902). The vessel in the centre is a Bucknall steamer, while the tug at the bow of the outside sailing vessel is one of an early class which had its lifeboats in davits on the foredeck, an arrangement that must have been extremely inconvenient for harbour work.

2 The tug *Danie du Plessis* in Durban Bay. She was among the first tugs to be built in South African yards in recent times.

3 Durban's Point wharves, early this century. A ship which could be the four-masted Union-Castle intermediate liner *Braemar Castle* is left of centre; astern of her is an early Blue Anchor Line vessel. A later ship belonging to this company, the *Waratah*, disappeared without trace near Port St Johns in 1909.

4 The *Ilderton* at Congella in October 1906, the first steamer to berth there. Owing to the reconstruction and expansion of inland industry after the Anglo-

Boer War, there was a considerable increase in trade and a consequent lack of berths at the port, making it necessary for the ship to discharge her cargo of timber at the unfinished wharf. In the absence of cranes, her own gear had to be used.

5 Number 1 Pier. Over the past few years there has been a significant shift in the utilization of the wharves at Durban. The berths in the Point area, formerly the hub of activity, have not been used to a great extent recently; those at Maydon Wharf, Island View, Number 1 Pier, and of course the container terminal, have assumed increasing importance. Apart from the occasional call by cruise liners, the great passenger terminal on the T-jetty has been quiet. Activity there will be a little brisker now that regular passenger sailings have been reintroduced.

1 Durban's container terminal. Today's facilities at the harbour are a far cry from the timber and stone jetties where sailing ships berthed, or the rough and ready wharves in use when the *Armadale Castle* became the first Union-Castle mailship to cross the bar in 1904. Whereas the barrels, boxes and bales of earlier times were all trundled by hand, most of today's cargoes are hidden in containers and the whole process is one of automated swiftness. Indeed, although Safmarine's *S.A. Winterberg*, seen here, has almost four times the cargo capacity of the old liners, it can be loaded or unloaded in far less time. Across the bay from the container terminal lies Maydon Wharf, where bulk cargo depots handle products ranging from sugar to manganese, maize to soda ash, groundnuts to molasses. Elsewhere in the bay there are coal berths, pig-iron loaders, pre-cooling sheds, oil terminals, phosphate and wood-chip depots, and shipyards.

2 Evening departure in the mailship days.

3 The mud flats of Durban Bay at low tide. With the swirl of currents and the wash from ships' propellers the sandbanks tend to move, making dredging permanently necessary.

4 The spreaders in the stacking area of the coal terminal at Richard's Bay.
5 Loading the coal. The degree of automation at Richard's Bay is remarkable.

THE DECISION TO develop the vast, natural lagoon at Richard's Bay was made for several reasons: because of an expected increase in trade, particularly in bulk commodities; because of the congestion at Durban during the economic boom of the late 1960s, a problem which was compounded by the closure of the Suez Canal; and, most important of all, because of a contract to export millions of tons of coal each year to Japan. After three years of construction the harbour was commissioned during an impressive ceremony in 1976, when the *S.A. Vaal* and various naval vessels came through the channel. In addition to the coal berths, other facilities have been provided to enable the port to handle most of the commodities produced and required by the industries at Richard's Bay ∎

A Minister-class strike craft of the South African Navy.

CHAPTER
III
THE NAVAL TRADITION

1

F ROM 1806 TO THE MID-1970s the Royal Navy maintained a permanent presence in South Africa, its traditions and operational techniques providing a model for the initial development of the South African Navy. In the earlier years of their presence, vessels of the Royal Navy moved troops and equipment to the Eastern Frontier of the Cape Colony during the periodic frontier wars. The Cape station was also a base from which naval action against West and East African slave-trading was conducted. Later,

when British forces clashed with the Boers in 1842, HMS *Southampton* provided covering gunfire for the landing of troops at Port Natal.

During the Anglo-Boer War scores of naval and commandeered vessels caused massive congestion at Cape Town and Durban. Ships were double- and triple-banked as they discharged troops and military cargo. Special colliers brought Welsh and Tyneside coal to bunker the transports in South African harbours. Boer prisoners were shipped in

2

crowded vessels to places of exile such as St Helena, the West Indies and Ceylon ■

1 Vice-Admiral George Keith Elphinstone (later First Viscount Keith) commanded the British naval force that captured a Dutch fleet at the Battle of Saldanha in 1795. Shortly thereafter he landed troops on the False Bay coast who succeeded in taking the Cape from the Dutch. The British occupation was a temporary move to prevent the French from capturing the Cape, and in 1803 the territory was handed back to the Dutch. Three years later, however, a British fleet under Commodore (later Admiral) Sir Home Riggs Popham brought troops who recaptured the Cape in a minor skirmish at Blaauwberg on the shores of Table Bay.

2 Seen here in February 1852 during her second visit to the Cape, HM Paddle Steamer *Birkenhead* approaches Simonstown. Three days later, carrying troops and some of their families, she headed for the eastern Cape, where the Eighth Frontier War had begun. Early on the morning of 26 February 1852 she ran aground on a reef at Danger Point. Her bottom was ripped open and she sank in rough water, the soldiers on board displaying remarkable bravery and devotion to duty. Out of 630 people on board, only 192 survived.

3 The Vice-Admiral's cutter comes ashore in Simon's Bay. In

the background is his flagship, HMS *Hermes,* a cruiser which was sunk in 1914 by *U-27* off the Ruylingen Bank.

4 Built in 1892, HMS *St George* is seen here in Table Bay harbour. She spent the First World War as a depot ship and was scrapped in 1920.

1 The requisitioned passenger steamer *Lake Manitoba* in Table Bay during the Anglo-Boer War. She brought troops and their equipment to South Africa.

2 Troops arriving aboard the *Braemar Castle,* which had been built for Donald Currie in Glasgow in 1898. Her role as a troopship did not end with the Peace of Vereeniging, for in 1909 she was taken over by the Admiralty and served as one of their fleet of peacetime troopers. During the First World War she was mined off the British coast while operating as a hospital ship. After repairs had been effected she took part in the North Russian campaign. Her post-war career was spent trooping for the Admiralty, apart

5

4

6

from a brief spell on the South
African run for her previous
owners. In 1924 she went to
Italian shipbreakers.

3 Field guns being landed for use
in the Anglo-Boer War.

4 A view across Green Point
Common during the Anglo-Boer
War. The ships in Table Bay are
mostly military transports and
include three Union-Castle
liners. The tents next to the cycle
track accommodated Boer
prisoners of war awaiting
transportation to St Helena and
elsewhere. Other tents were for
the military personnel guarding
the prisoners or for troops
awaiting dispatch to the war
fronts.

5 The relief of Ladysmith on 28
February 1900 was a cause for
great rejoicing because the town
had been besieged by Boer forces
for months. The photograph
shows vessels at Durban's Point
wharves dressed overall to
celebrate the occasion. The
shortage of berths as a result of
the armada of military
transports in South African
harbours is well illustrated here
by the triple-banking of vessels.
One of the ships is a Bullard
King liner, perhaps the second
Umtata or the first *Umgeni*.

6 The *City of Cambridge* came to
South Africa with troops in 1901.
While in Cape waters she stood
by HMS *Sybille,* which was
wrecked near Lambert's Bay in
January of that year.

AFTER 1885 SIMON'S BAY became an exclusive anchorage of the Royal Navy. The Anglo-Boer War and the ominous naval build-up in Germany precipitated the construction of a proper naval base, including a tidal basin and dry dock. In 1910 the Simonstown docks were opened and became the principal harbour for vessels of the Cape of Good Hope and West Coast of Africa Station (later renamed the South Atlantic Station). After the declaration of war in 1914 there was a dislocation of regular shipping services to and from South Africa as ships were commandeered, re-routed or lost as a result of hostilities. The campaign to capture German South West Africa saw many British liners and local coasters pressed into service as transports or even escorts. In Table Bay harbour and at Simonstown familar ships were fitted out for the campaign, which involved landing British and South African troops at Walvis Bay, Lüderitzbucht and Port Nolloth.

At the end of the campaign, in 1915, many of the requisitioned vessels were dispatched elsewhere.

German surface raiders, such as the *Kaiser Wilhelm der Grosse* or the very successful former merchantman *Wolf,* made life for the South Atlantic Squadron extremely difficult. Apart from the hazards created by their minelaying activities, there was a constant threat of direct attacks by the raiders on British shipping. From the early days of the war, convoys therefore had to be provided with escorts, such as those for the convoy carrying the Imperial Garrison from South Africa to Southampton in August 1914 – a convoy which included five Union-Castle liners. To aggravate the security situation in South African waters, all vessels moving between Britain and the Eastern Hemisphere were diverted via the Cape because the Mediterranean was unsafe. The vessels of the Royal Navy had their work cut out to ensure the safety of this volume of shipping, and the South African port authorities were

faced with severe congestion in harbours which at that time had only limited berthing accommodation and communication systems. After 1919 the South Atlantic Station returned to its peacetime role, the Commander-in-Chief and his senior officers resuming the civic and social engagements which were such a hallmark of the Royal Naval presence in South Africa ■

1 HMS *Good Hope,* which was sunk on 1 November 1914 during the Battle of Coronel off the coast of Chile. Her armour and her two 230-mm and sixteen 150-mm guns were no match for the broadsides fired by the German ships *Scharnhorst* and *Gneisenau.*

2 The *Rufidji,* a Deutsche Ost-Afrika Linie vessel, was captured off the Cape Peninsula on 18 August 1914. She was renamed *Huntscliff* and was lost in the North Atlantic in 1918.

3 The Union-Castle liner *Kinfauns Castle* at anchor off Simonstown in 1914. As an armed merchant cruiser she participated in the South West African campaign and in the hunt for the German cruiser *Königsberg* along the East African coast.

4 HMS *Good Hope* leaving Table Bay harbour in November 1908. She was the flagship of the Second Cruiser Squadron, whose other vessels were HMS *Antrim,* HMS *Carnarvon* and HMS *Devonshire.* In the photograph the last two vessels are in the bay.

1

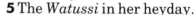

2

1 The German raider *Atlantis*, seen here disguised as a two-funneller, was perhaps the most successful of all the raiders.

2 To refuel and revictual their submarines and surface raiders in the South Atlantic, a number of supply ships were sent out by the Germans. One such was the *Python*, which rescued the survivors of the *Atlantis* but was herself scuttled to avoid capture by HMS *Dorsetshire* a week later.

3 Caught at sea off the East African coast as war loomed in August 1939, the Deutsche Ost-Afrika Linie passenger liner *Watussi* put into harbour in Mozambique. In November 1939 she broke out, disguised as a Union-Castle ship. Sighted by an aircraft of the South African Air Force on 2 December while off Cape Point, she was ordered to steer for Simonstown. But when the cruiser HMS *Sussex* approached her later in the day she was abandoned by her crew and scuttled.

4 HMS *Swale*, a River-class frigate, which was based in South African waters for a period during the Second World War. Many South Africans served in her; indeed, from August 1945 to January 1946 the ship was manned by a SANF crew.

5 The *Watussi* in her heyday.

IN SEPTEMBER 1939 an unparalleled devastation of shipping began. As in 1914, regular shipping services ceased; popular liners were painted grey and, in most cases, their lavish interiors were stripped. Some vessels became armed merchant cruisers in preparation for a prolonged and savage maritime struggle, which was brought home to South Africans not only by the frequent announcements of the loss of well-known liners in the major theatres of war, but also by the success of German surface raiders and submarines along the Cape sea route. More than 160 ships were torpedoed or sunk by mines or naval guns within 1 000 nautical miles of the coastline ■

3

AGAIN THE CONVOYS came, this time in greater numbers and including larger ships. On a number of occasions about forty ships lay in the roadsteads of Table Bay and Durban. In addition to these two harbours, a third submarine-proof harbour for convoys was established at Saldanha Bay. Troops from many different nations passed this way, while South African troops travelled to East Africa, to Red Sea ports, or even to Europe, in liners from other trades. Cunarders, the Empresses, P. and O. liners, and others such as the *Ile de France* and the *Nieuw Amsterdam,* slipped into South African ports during those dark days when talk about ships and shipping was taboo. One of these unusual callers, the Orient liner *Orcades,* was sunk by *U-172* about 250 nautical miles WSW of Cape Point on 10 October 1942 ■

1 The *Aquitania* on a wartime visit to Table Bay. She was refuelled and revictualled in the roadstead. Her four raked funnels, her counter stern and her well-proportioned superstructure made her one of the most impressive liners to call. She survived the war and was scrapped in 1950, the last of the world's great four-funnellers.
2 The departure for North Africa of a battalion of the Royal Durban Light Infantry. Scenes like this were common, particularly during the early years of the war. Those involved will remember the overwhelming grief of friends and family and the turmoil in the minds of the soldiers as they embarked.
3 South African troops aboard the Union-Castle liner

called at South African ports several times, mainly carrying Australian troops to the front line. The *Australia* was a cruiser, built in 1927 and armed with eight 200-mm and four 100-mm guns. She was scrapped in 1955.

GREAT NUMBERS of South Africans went to sea in defence of their country and the Empire, and served with distinction in ships of the Royal Navy, the merchant navy or the hastily revised Seaward Defence Force, later known as the South African Naval Forces. But occasionally South African homes were shattered by the arrival of the chaplain or the local priest to tell of the sinking of a fine ship – the *Barham*, the *Dorsetshire*, the *Cornwall*, or another – for among those lost in these ships there were South African lads, seconded to the Royal Navy, as well as their British 'oppos' ∎

Llanstephan Castle. The sandbags around the bridge and the after gun emplacement can be seen, while the lifeboats are swung out of their davits because of the threat of attack by submarines.
4 The Cunarders *Queen Mary* and *Aquitania* at anchor off Simonstown during the war, probably in 1940.
5 HMAS *Australia* leads the *Queen Mary* and the *Aquitania* as they leave Simonstown for Europe via Freetown in 1940. These two North Atlantic liners

1 The *Queen Mary* in her wartime guise under the shadow of Table Mountain.

2 The great Cunarder *Queen Elizabeth* also paid several visits to South African ports during the Second World War. On one occasion (May 1942) she anchored off Simonstown to embark hundreds of prisoners of war captured during the North African campaign and brought to South Africa in smaller vessels. A contemporary newspaper article reported that a number of these prisoners had attempted to escape by jumping overboard, either from the tugs and tenders taking them out to the ship or from the liner herself, and that some of them had drowned in the attempt. Throughout the war years her speed (32 knots maximum) and her capacity to carry thousands of troops made her a singularly useful vessel.

In 1946 she began her regular North Atlantic crossings. She had been completed only in 1940 and had therefore made no voyages for Cunard before the outbreak of war. She was withdrawn from service in 1968 and was to become a floating convention centre in Florida, but was purchased two years later by the Chinese shipowner C.Y. Tung, who planned to use her as a floating university. Thus it was that in June 1971 she made her last call in Table Bay harbour, where, as the *Seawise University*, she docked to take on bunkers before steaming to Hong Kong to be refitted. About seven months later she caught fire at her Hong Kong anchorage and was completely destroyed. So ended the career of the largest passenger liner (in terms of tonnage).

3 HMAMC *Carnarvon Castle* enters Table Bay harbour after her unsuccessful engagement with the German raider *Thor* in December 1940 (see page 85). Damage was fairly extensive and temporary repairs were effected in Montevideo.

and the *Aronda*, had magnificent teak bridges, something unheard of in modern shipbuilding.

7 Rendered harmless by naval explosives experts, this gift from a German raider is removed from a Cape beach. To counter the threat of mines, trawlers and whalers were converted into minesweepers.

4 Shell and shrapnel damage to the promenade deck of the *Carnarvon Castle*.

5 The popular Bullard King liner *Umgeni* entering Port Elizabeth harbour in the final stages of the war. Her armaments, life-rafts and protected bridge are evident. With her sister ships, the *Umtali* and the *Umtata*, she had operated a one-class passenger service between South Africa and Britain before the war. The *Umtata* was a war casualty, lost in 1942 off the coast of Florida. The other two ships resumed service after the war and in 1957 were sold to Elder Dempster Lines for the West African trade.

6 One of the few uncensored wartime harbour photographs shows the hospital ship *Amra* in Durban. Her post-war service from India to East and South Africa brought her to Durban frequently, until her scrapping in 1966. She and her two sister ships, the *Aska* (sunk in 1940)

1 HMS *Howe,* seen here in Durban harbour, was one of the largest warships to visit South African ports during the war. She was laid down as the *Beatty* in 1937 but was completed only in August 1942. The following year she was in action at the Sicilian operations and at Salerno. Just before the end of the war she was transferred to the Pacific, her voyage taking her via South Africa. She was scrapped in 1958.

2 HMS *Neptune* came from the builders' yard in 1933. In 1939 the Commander-in-Chief South Atlantic, Vice-Admiral G.H. D'Oyly Lyon, flew his flag in her. By June 1940 she was with the Mediterranean Fleet and was mined off Tripoli in 1941. Eighteen South Africans seconded to the Royal Navy were serving in her at the time. Only one member of the ship's company survived.

3 The convoys came and went. This one, in 1941, included vessels from all the great passenger lines. Union-Castle was represented by the *Capetown Castle,* the *Carnarvon Castle* and one of the fruit ships, but there were P. and O. liners, Canadian Pacific ships, and others. The average monthly total of ships (excluding warships) that called at South African ports while in transit reached about 230. The total for 1942, the busiest year, was 3 858 transit vessels.

4 Ten 360-mm and sixteen 130-mm guns formed the main armament of HMS *Prince of*

Wales, which visited Table Bay in November 1941, just six months after her action with the *Bismarck.* Previously she had carried Winston Churchill to meet President Roosevelt 'somewhere in the Atlantic'. But just a month after her call at Cape Town she was sunk by Japanese aircraft. Her consort, HMS *Repulse,* was also lost in the same attack. Admiral Sir Tom Phillips, Commander-in-Chief Eastern Fleet, and Captain J. C. Leach, captain of HMS

Prince of Wales, who had entertained newsmen and others aboard the *Prince of Wales* while she was in Cape Town, were lost with the ship on 10 December 1941.

5 The German submarine *U-178* returning to her base in Bordeaux, France on 9 January 1943 after a sortie off the Southern African seaboard, during which she had sunk three Allied ships and damaged the Harrison freighter *Adviser.* In April of that year she again

ventured into South African waters and between the end of May and mid-July had dispatched a further six vessels. Thereafter she went to Penang for a refit, but after some delay at that port she returned to Europe, adding another victim en route. During her action off the local seaboard she was attacked twice by South African aircraft but escaped unscathed. To avoid capture by the invasion forces she was scuttled in Bordeaux in August 1944.

1

3

2

IN THE POST-WAR period, with the South African Navy growing, the Royal Navy began a process of gradual disengagement in this part of the world. In April 1957 the Simonstown naval base was handed over to South Africa and the Royal Naval squadron withdrew, leaving a token force on the South Atlantic Station.

However, the old days were revived during periodic exercises with the South African Navy, as it was customary for the Royal Navy to provide a number of ships, even aircraft carriers, for the exercises. Simonstown and other ports were swamped when the sailors of the Royal Navy hit town again. For political reasons the joint exercises eventually

ceased, and in 1976 the White Ensign was hauled down for the last time and the Royal Navy decommissioned its shore establishment, HMS *Afrikander*. Admiralty House, the gracious Royal Naval residence on Wynberg Hill in Cape Town, now serves as a conference centre for a leading insurance company.

The presence of the Royal

Navy at the Cape for nearly 200 years established a strong naval tradition at the southern tip of Africa. It was on this foundation that the South African Navy was built ■

1 Vice-Admirals Tottenham and Evans at Admiralty House in Simonstown in September 1935 when Tottenham succeeded Evans as Commander-in-Chief South Atlantic. Evans is renowned as 'Evans of the *Broke*', a nickname he earned through his outstanding command of a British destroyer squadron which engaged six German destroyers in the English Channel in April 1917.
2 The cruiser HMS *Amphion* enters the Selborne Dry Dock in Simonstown in 1936 during her period as flagship, South Atlantic Station. She was sold to Australia and, as HMAS *Perth*, was torpedoed in the Sunda Straits in March 1942.
3 HMS *Vanguard*, the last

British battleship to be built and the last to visit South African ports, is seen here during the royal tour of South Africa in 1947.
4 The nuclear powered submarine HMS *Dreadnought* enters Simonstown shortly before the final British withdrawal from South Africa.
5 One of the last British

warships based at the Cape was HMS *Puma,* a *Leopard*-class frigate.
6 The last British Vice-Admiral to command the South Atlantic Station, Vice-Admiral J.M.D. Gray, left the Cape in April 1967 and was succeeded by a Commodore. In March 1976 all Royal Naval personnel were withdrawn.

the Suez Canal, a fact which illustrates the importance of the Cape sea route as the only viable alternative to the Canal ■

OVER THE YEARS many foreign warships have visited South African ports on courtesy calls, or for joint naval exercises with the South African Navy, or for bunkering and revictualling. Such calls, particularly those by major warships, generated great interest among the South African public, who queued for hours to be able to board the ships. Most of Britain's aircraft carriers were here at one time or another, notably during the period of the Royal Navy's permanent presence at the Cape and during the two closures of

1 One of the most notable German naval callers to Southern Africa between the wars was the light cruiser *Karlsruhe,* built in 1927, seen here at anchor off Lüderitz in 1930. A training ship until 1935, she joined the main fleet and was so badly damaged by three torpedoes during the Norwegian invasion that her crew scuttled her.
2 Entering Table Bay harbour in 1934 is the German cruiser *Emden,* whose main armaments were eight 150-mm guns. Lawrence Green recorded that he had met Karl Dönitz on her during this call.
3 The German training ship *Schulschiff Deutschland,* making a courtesy call at Cape Town in the early 1930s. She carried almost 200 cadets, and over the years provided training in seamanship for some prominent German naval officers.
4 A more recent training ship to visit these parts was the Chilean vessel *Esmeralda.* Other sailing vessels of this kind to call at South African ports included the Brazilian *Almirante Saldanha,* the Spanish *Juan Sebastian de el*

4

5

6

Cano, the Argentinian *Libertad* and the Columbian *Gloria.*

5 The aircraft carrier USS *Franklin D. Roosevelt* put into Cape Town en route from the Far East to the United States in February 1967. The visit turned sour when shore leave for the officers and ratings was cancelled owing to political problems involving the presence of Negro crewmen aboard the ship. Apparently the South African authorities had agreed to the visit with no strings attached, and it was alleged at the time that the problems had originated on the American side.

During the shortened stay (three days instead of four) the vessel's crew were impressed by the reaction of the local people, and the commander issued a statement thanking all those whose offers of hospitality had had to be refused. This was the last visit to South African ports by a major American warship. United States cruisers and the sister ship to the *Franklin D. Roosevelt,* the *Midway,* had previously been here.

6 Many British aircraft carriers docked in South African ports in the days of the Royal Navy's permanent presence and during

the subsequent joint exercises with the South African Navy. Apart from HMS *Victorious,* seen here on her visit in February 1961, HMS *Bulwark,* HMS *Warrior,* HMS *Albion,* HMS *Eagle* and others also called. Their arrival in South African ports was always a great occasion, with thousands of spectators turning out to watch the vessels and their escorts tie up. HMS *Victorious* was built in 1941 and reconstructed from 1950 to 1958, emerging from the dockyard in Portsmouth with a very different appearance. She was scrapped in 1969.

In 1861 the first local naval unit, the Port Elizabeth Naval Volunteer Brigade, was formed, but it lasted only a short time. Twenty-four years later the Bluff Battery in Durban was manned by the newly-formed Natal Naval Volunteers, a unit which served ashore in the Anglo-Boer War (1899-1902) and in the Zulu Rebellion (1906). The NNV and a similar unit, the Cape Naval Volunteers, merged to form the Royal Naval Volunteer Reserve (S.A.) in 1913, which saw service at sea in the First World War.

A fully-fledged South African naval force became a reality only in January 1922, when the country's first naval vessels arrived from Britain and anchored in Simon's Bay. These were the survey ship HMSAS *Protea* (ex HMS *Crozier*), HMSAS *Immortelle* (ex HMS *Foyle,* an Admiralty trawler) and her sister ship, HMSAS *Sonneblom* (ex HMS *Eden*). Manned by a new arm of the South African Defence Force, the South African Naval Service, these ships were used for hydrographic work and naval training. During the great depression the ships were disposed of and, apart from a skeleton staff, the men were paid off. However, four RNVR (SA) bases continued to operate.

It took the Second World War to resuscitate a naval force, the Seaward Defence Force, which was amalgamated with the RNVR (SA) to form the South African Naval Forces on 1 August 1942. To counter the threat from both submarines and surface raiders, sixty-five whalers and trawlers were armed and equipped with minesweeping gear and anti-submarine weaponry. For a variety of other tasks, craft such as tugs and coasters were requisitioned by the Admiralty and manned by South Africans.

3 Converted whalers formed part of the SANF during the Second World War. HMSAS *Benoni* (T54), HMSAS *Southern Barrier* (T28) and HMSAS *Brakpan* (T42) are berthed in Cape Town's Alfred Basin.

4 SAS *Good Hope,* a *Loch*-class frigate, was launched in 1944 and spent her wartime days on convoy escort and on patrol in the Western Approaches. She became the flagship of the South African Navy and an extensive refit saw Admiral's quarters added to the afterdeck. After becoming redundant in the late 1960s she was laid up, prior to being scuttled in False Bay.

5 SAS *Natal,* another *Loch*-class frigate, was undergoing sea trials off St Abb's Head in March 1945 when she sank the German submarine *U-714.* Her captain, Lieutenant-Commander D.A. Hall, was awarded a bar to his DSC, which had been won in the *Southern Maid* in the Mediterranean in 1941. Later she was used as a survey ship until replaced by SAS *Protea* in 1971. The third of the *Loch*-class trio, SAS *Transvaal,* carried the annexation party to Marion Island and Prince Edward Island in 1947.

A flotilla of anti-submarine vessels, minesweepers and a salvage ship went to the Mediterranean, where four were lost through enemy action. South African naval personnel were awarded 225 decorations ■

1 HMSAS *Sonneblom.*
2 Heaving the lead (i.e. measuring the depth of the sea) aboard the first HMSAS *Protea.* There have been three other ships of that name in South African naval history: an ex-whaler which did service in the Mediterranean (1941-1946); an ex-corvette which was used as a survey ship (1947-1962); and SAS *Protea,* a vessel of the Royal Navy's *Hecla*-class, built in Glasgow in 1971.

1 SAS *Protea,* formerly the
corvette HMS *Rockrose,* was the
Navy's hydrographic survey ship
from 1947 to 1962.
2 Admiral H.H. Biermann, SSA,
SD, OBE, the first South African
to achieve the rank of Admiral in
the South African Defence Force.
3 Five of the men who played a
great part in shaping the South
African Navy. Left to right:
Lieutenant-Commander (later
Rear-Admiral) S.C. Biermann,
wearing the old sleeve insignia of
an Instructor-Officer;
Commodore (later Admiral) H.H.
Biermann, OBE; Commodore
F.J. ('Dizzy') Dean, OBE, a

5

former Chief of the SANF; Captain (later Commodore) H.E. Fougstedt; Commander J. ('Flam') Johnson, DSC, (later Vice-Admiral and Chief of the Navy).

4 Two destroyers, SAS *Jan van Riebeeck* (ex HMS *Wessex*) and (shown here) SAS *Simon van der Stel* (ex HMS *Whelp*) joined the fleet in 1950 and 1952 respectively, prior to which they had been in the Royal Naval reserve fleet at Simonstown. Between 1962 and 1966 each vessel underwent considerable modification, including the construction of a helicopter deck and hangar. In the early 1970s

both were laid up and later became targets for testing various kinds of weaponry.

5 One of the Navy's mine countermeasures vessels. There are ten modified vessels of the Royal Navy's Ton-class coastal minesweepers in the fleet. All bear the names of South African towns.

6 Gunnery practice aboard a President-class frigate.

7 SAS *President Kruger,* the first of three frigates of the Royal Navy's *Rothesay*-class to be built in British yards between 1959 and 1964 as part of the joint South African-British strategy

6

for the defence of the Cape sea route. All three were refitted in the late 1960s and equipped with the most modern anti-submarine and anti-aircraft systems. A helicopter hangar and flight deck were also installed. SAS *President Steyn* has been laid up while SAS *President Kruger* was lost after a tragic collision with the fleet replenishment ship SAS *Tafelberg* in 1982. SAS *President Pretorius* is still in commission. Her main armaments include twin 115-mm guns, 40-mm anti-aircraft Bofors, anti-submarine mortars and torpedoes, and Wasp helicopters.

7

F150

IN APRIL 1957 the developing navy, which had assumed the name South African Navy in 1951, took over control of Simonstown from the Royal Navy and expansion followed. Until the termination of a joint defence agreement (the so-called Simonstown Agreement) by Britain in 1975, there had been close co-operation on naval matters between South Africa and Whitehall. Indeed, the South African Navy possessed a

number of former Royal Naval vessels, and three *Rothesay*-class frigates had been specially built for South Africa in British yards.

After the termination of the Simonstown Agreement, French yards supplied three *Daphne*-class submarines, but the subsequent failure of France to honour contracts for corvettes and additional submarines has led to the construction of naval vessels by local shipbuilders, a development which has secured both the future supply of warships and the future of the South African shipbuilding industry.

Strike craft, submarines and mine countermeasures vessels presently form the bulk of the navy's muscle at sea, while extremely sophisticated naval armaments, tracking systems, communications networks and other equipment provide the necessary back-up. In addition to Simonstown, the navy has advanced bases at Durban and Walvis Bay and support facilities at other harbours, enabling it to operate freely and effectively along the entire coastline of South Africa ■

1 SAS *President Pretorius* refuelling from SAS *Tafelberg*. The latter vessel has recently undergone a refit, which includes the facility to carry and deploy large helicopters. In her new role she will be able to assist in airsea rescue operations when the ageing Shackleton aircraft of the South African Air Force are phased out.
2 Following the abrogation by Britain of the Simonstown

Agreement for the joint defence of the Cape sea route and South Africa, British yards would not accept orders for South African naval vessels. French yards were therefore contracted to build three *Daphne*-class submarines, SAS *Maria van Riebeeck*, SAS *Emily Hobhouse* and SAS *Johanna van der Merwe*, which were delivered in 1971/2. These vessels have subsequently been modified and updated in Simonstown, and plans to construct submarines locally have been announced.
3 The French cancellation of orders for the building of corvettes forced the South African Navy to make alternative arrangements, and strike craft from local yards soon took to the water. The extremely accurate guided-missile systems of these Minister-class craft, and their· capacity for high speed, make them a potent maritime force.
4 Since the Second World War, air-sea rescue launches have been stationed along the South African coast. The present base for these vessels, SAS *Flamingo,* is located on the Langebaan lagoon near Saldanha. In the photograph the launches exercise on the lagoon.
5 SAS *President Steyn* in her heyday.

THE GENERAL BOTHA

In memory of his son who was killed in the First World War, Mr Thomas B.F. Davis bought and presented to the South African Government in 1921 the obsolete cruiser HMS *Thames,* for use as a nautical training ship. After a refit the vessel was anchored in Simon's Bay as the SATS *General Botha.* Life for the lads aboard was tough, owing to extremely tight discipline. On leaving the 'Bothie', as she was affectionately known, the cadets usually took apprenticeships with British shipping lines or joined SAR ships as deckhands for the voyages to load railway sleepers in Australia. During the Second World War the boys moved to barracks on Red Hill at Simonstown, but in 1946 the ship was found to be in need of too much repair and new quarters for a stone training ship were commissioned at Gordon's Bay. The old ship was scuttled in False Bay.

The South African Shipowners' Association and the Department of National Education later took over control of merchant naval training, and in 1966 the South African Merchant Naval Academy *General Botha* opened at Granger Bay in Cape Town.

Nautical training has evolved considerably over the years. Gone are the two years at the training ship as well as the subsequent one-year post-school course. Now prospective officers proceed straight to sea after their normal schooling and attend a course at the *General Botha* as part of their training, and can write the examination for their Second Mate's Certificate shortly

1 President-class frigates illuminated for the Republic festival in 1971.
2 SATS *General Botha* sinking in False Bay in 1947.
3 SATS *General Botha* in Simon's Bay.
4 The modern nautical academy *General Botha* at Granger Bay.

thereafter. Courses for other navigating certificates are also offered. The para-naval discipline in merchant naval training has gone forever.

But the tradition and accomplishments of the old 'Bothie' are remembered by many. A number of senior naval officers received their initial maritime training there (Admiral Hugo Biermann, among others), as did most of the top technical management in the South African merchant navy and the Harbour Service ■

1

2

THE PASSENGER service to Southern Africa commenced in the seventeenth century when the Dutch East India Company established a supply station at the Cape to provision ships travelling to and from the East. During the next one and a half centuries, Company officials, settlers and slaves were conveyed to the Cape in a variety of sailing vessels. There was a considerable increase in passenger traffic after the second occupation of the Cape by the British in 1806, when government officials and military personnel came out to administer the territory. This was followed by the arrival of British settlers, most notably those who sailed in the *Chapman* and other ships to Algoa Bay in 1820.

The demand for additional berths between England and the Cape developed into a lucrative business for the many shipowners who put their vessels on the route. As colonization spread to the eastern Cape and to Natal, coastal passenger services also began. Direct sailings from England to ports other than Cape Town were introduced, involving, among others, the Natal Direct Line. Indeed, at all ports and anchorages immigrants arrived to begin a new life in a part of the world which was very different from their places of origin. For all of them even the outward voyage was an arduous affair, lasting several months ■

CHAPTER
IV
PASSENGER SERVICES

1 Aboard the *Roslin Castle*, a steamer on the mail service from 1883 to 1904.
2 The *Windsor Castle* on her maiden voyage in 1960. The second-last Union-Castle passenger mailship to be built, she was the largest in terms of her accommodation (over 800 passengers) and length (239 metres). She was the last Union-Castle passenger mailship in service, and when she departed in 1977 an era in South Africa's maritime history came to an end.

THE CAPE OF GOOD HOPE AND PORT NATAL

Shipping and Mercantile Gazette.

VOL. XVI.] CAPE TOWN, FRIDAY, JULY 6, 1860. No. 861.

To Merchants

AND ALL OTHER PARTIES CONCERNED.

LLOYDS' INSTRUCTIONS

Regarding Damaged Goods by Sea Water.

1ST.—The Goods to be surveyed *immediately* after landing, by two Merchants, conversant with the particular description of Goods, who shall in their Certificate specify the *quantity damaged and the quantity sound in each package*, and the nature of the damage, they shall also, in cases where actual Cash Sales cannot be produced, certify the Cash Market Price of the said Goods, where they are in a sound state, but shall not allow a per centage on Invoice value.

2nd.—The Master of the Vessel from which the Goods have been received, to be called on to the above survey and to certify the nature and cause of the damage.

It is also agreed that the Underwriters will be held liable for the particular average loss on the

Damaged Pieces only in each Package;

these Pieces to be selected from the sound, and sold by Auction, or otherwise.

WM. DICKSON & Co., Agents for Lloyds.

Underwriters' Room, Liverpool, 4th Feb., 1854.

THIS IS TO CERTIFY to all whom it may concern that the Committee for Managing the Affairs of the "LIVERPOOL UNDERWRITERS' ASSOCIATION" have appointed

Messrs. James Searight & Co.

to act as their Agents at Cape Town and the Vicinity

(Signed) THOS. COURT, Sec.

THE Undersigned hereby notify that they have accepted the above Trust, and that they are in possession of full instructions to act on all occasions in which the Liverpool Underwriters' Association may be interested. J. SEARIGHT & Co.

Freight and Passage to England

BY THE

ROYAL MAIL STEAM-SHIPS

THE Union Steam-ship Company's fine Steam-ship NORMAN, JOHN BOXER, Commander, is appointed to leave Table Bay with Her Majesty's Mails (calling at St. Helena and Ascension) on the 21st day of July, and will be due in England on the 1st day of September.—Apply to the Company's Agents,

WM. ANDERSON, SAXON, & Co.

For Freight or Charter.

THE A 1 Brig BLUE JACKET, 200 Tons Register, W. MOORE, Master, is open for Freight or Charter to any part of the World.

Sails well and carries a large Cargo.—Apply to

PRINCE, COLLISON, & Co.

For East London.

THE A 1 Brig QUEEN, Capt. WILKES, will be ready to receive Cargo THIS DAY; has also accommodations for Passengers.—Apply to

THOMSON, WATSON, & Co.

No goods received on board without an order.

For Port Elizabeth.

THE fine fast-sailing Schooner REINHARDT, Capt. BECKELBACH, will, upon discharge of her inward Cargo fill up for the above Port, and having part Cargo, for there, will be dispatched without delay.—For Freight or Passage, apply to

DEANE & JOHNSON.

For Mauritius.

THE Clipper Bark SPIRIT OF THE AGE, TAYLOR, Master, will, on discharge of part of her Cargo for this port, proceed as above, taking such Freight as may offer. JAMES SEARIGHT & Co.

NOW LANDING,

EX

"WEST INDIAN,"

Crushed Sugar
Pearl Barley
Split Peas
Edwards' Preserved Potatoes
Candles
White and Red Lead
Boiled Oil, 2-gallon tins
Green Paint
Blue „
Assorted „
Patent Castile Paint
Venetian Red
Celestial Blue
Finest Prussian Blue
Do. Verdigris
(in 1, 2, and 3-lb. jars)
Putty
Turpentine, 2-gallon tins
Glue
Brimstone
Ultramarine Stone Blue
Stone Blue
Copal Varnish, 1-gallon tins
Sheet Lead, 4, 5, 6, lb.
Lead Piping, ½ and ¾ Inch
Composition Piping, ¼, ½, and ¾
Patent Shot, Nos. 1 @ 6.

H. E. RUTHERFOORD & BROTHER.

RICE.

THE Undersigned are landing ex *Deane*, from Calcutta,

WHITE AND BROWN RICE
TAMARINDS, RATTANS
INDIAN CURRY POWDER, &c.

DEANE & JOHNSON.

SALE OF THE WRECKED BARK

"SIR HENRY POTTINGER,"

CAPTAIN GUEST.

This Day (Friday, 6th instant),

AT TWO O'CLOCK P.M. MR. JONES WILL SELL,

The Hull of the above Vessel,

AS SHE NOW LIES ON THE BEACH AT SALT RIVER, TOGETHER WITH HER Tackle, Apparel, Anchors and Cables, Spars, Boats, Water Casks, Stores, &c., as may remain on board at the time of Sale,

FOR AND ON ACCOUNT OF THE UNDERWRITERS, OR WHOM IT MAY CONCERN.

ROBERT GRANGER & Co., Agents.

P. SHENTON & Co.

HAVE FOR SALE,

At their Stores, 74, Longmarket-street, the following Goods, received per late Arrivals:

Sardines, in ½ and ¼-tins
Belmont, Sperm, and other Candles
Confectionery, of all kinds
Sauces „
Worcester Sauce
Pickles
Mustard
Kippered Herrings
Fresh „
Red „
Bottled Fruits
Salad and Castor Oils
Fresh Salmon
Assorted Potted Meats
English Lard
Macaroni and Vermicelli
Anchovy and Bloater Paste
Teas, Sugars, &c.
Butter, of all kinds
Oysters and Lobsters
Jams and Jellies
Marmalade
Hams (York), in prime condition
Cheese, of all kinds
Filbert, Barcelona, Spanish, and Brazilian Nuts
Cocoa, Coffee, Chocolate, &c.
Prunes.

Ex Steamer "Celt:"

Hams, York and Westphalia
Bacon, Wiltshire, Hampshire, and Cumberland
Spiced Beef
Nuts, of all kinds
Assorted Sauces
Bottled Fruits
Fresh English Herrings
North Wiltshire Cheese
English Butter.

London and South African Bank.

TO BE INCORPORATED BY ROYAL CHARTER, WITH LIMITED LIABILITY.

Capital, £400,000, in 20,000 Shares of £20 each.

WITH POWER TO INCREASE.

ONE FOURTH OF THE SHARES WILL BE RESERVED FOR THE COLONY.

Deposit, £2 per Share, of which £1 must be paid upon application, and £1 upon allotment.

DIRECTORS.

JOHN BARRY, Esq., Messrs. BARRY & NEPHEWS, London and Cape Town.
THOMAS TYRINGHAM BERNARD, Esq., M.P., Director of the London and County Bank
PHILLIP PATTON BLYTH, Esq., Director of the London and County Bank.
JOHN HEGAN, Esq., 11, New Broad-street, London.
Colonel HOLLAND, Director of the Agra and United Service Bank.
JOHN HENRY LANCE, Esq., Director of the London and County Bank.
JOSEPH LEVICK, Esq., Messrs. LEVICKS & SHERMAN, London and Cape Town.
JOSEPH McMASTER, Esq., Messrs. McMASTER & CRUMP, London and Graham's Town.
CHARLES MAYNARD, Esq., Messrs. MAYNARD BROTHERS & Co., London, Port Elizabeth, and Graham's Town.
ADOLPHUS MOSENTHAL, Esq., Messrs. MOSENTHAL & Co., London, Port Elizabeth, and Cape Town.
WM. NICOL, Esq., M.P., Deputy Chairman of the Chartered Bank of India, Australia, and China.
JOHN ROBERT THOMSON, Esq., Messrs. J. R. Thomson & Co. London, Cape Town, and Port Elizabeth.

BANKERS.

LONDON AND COUNTY BANK.

SOLICITORS.

Messrs. WILKINSON, STEVENS, and WILKINSON, Nicholas-lane, Lombard-street.

SECRETARY.

JOHN A. MERINGTON, ESQ.

BROKERS.

Messrs. P. CAZENOVE and Co. 52, Threadneedle-street.
G. E. SEYMOUR, Esq., 38, Throgmorton-street.

TEMPORARY OFFICES.

GRESHAM HOUSE, 16, OLD BROAD-STREET, E.C.

THE FOLLOWING IS THE FORM OF APPLICATION.

APPLICATION FOR SHARES.

The Directors of the London and South African Bank.

Gentlemen,—I request that you will allot to me Shares in the London and South African Bank, or any less number, which I hereby accept, and agree to pay in addition to the sum of £ herewith sent, the several Instalments thereon as required, and to execute the necessary Deeds of Incorporation; and I also agree that if I do not pay the balance of the Deposit, the allotment may be cancelled and the Deposit forfeited.

Name in full.
Profession or Description.
Date.
Residence in full.

Applications to be made or addressed to Mr. JOHN BARRY, at the Office of Messrs. FAIRBRIDGE & HULL.

For Sale,

At the Stores of the Undersigned,

Caper and Orange Pekoe Tea
Mauritius Sugars
Ginger and Chow Chow Preserves
Camphorwood Trunks
White and Coloured Matting
American Clocks
Hams and Lard
Scales with English Weights, for 1860
Salmon, Mackerel
Spirits, Chairs of all descriptions
Tobacco, Leaf, 10 sticks and ½ lb. lumps
Hops (Sussex)
Sandoway Havannah Cigars
Imitation Manilla do.
White Rice, Tamarinds
Split Peas, Currants
Oilman's Stores
Wool and Grain Bags
Duck, Canvas, Hessian
Nails, Anvils, Blister and Cast Steel
Grubbing Hoes
Horse and Mule Shoes
Mould, Belmont Sperm, and Belmont Candles
Casey's Soap, 50 lb. and 56 lb. Boxes
Ale, in Bulk and Bottle
Wines and Spirits, do.
Portland Cement, &c., &c.

BORRADAILE, THOMPSON, HALL, & Co.

Blue Serge, Flannel, &c.

THE UNDERSIGNED have just received, and offer for Sale,

BLUE SERGE
FLANNELS
BLACK CLOTH; also
WOOLLEN SHAWLS.

BORRADAILE, THOMPSON, HALL, & Co.

Consignee Wanted,

FOR G. M.—100 Boxes CHEESE, landed from the *Reinhardt*. If not claimed, will be sold on account of the concerned.

DEANE & JOHNSON.

Cape Commercial Bank.

ANNUAL GENERAL MEETING.

NOTICE TO SHAREHOLDERS.

IN pursuance of the 24th and 26th Sections of the Deed of Settlement, Notice is hereby given that the Annual General Meeting will be held at the Banking-house, No. 36, Adderley-street, on

Saturday, the 7th July,

AT 11 O'CLOCK IN THE FORENOON,

for submitting to the Shareholders the Statement of the Affairs of the Bank and the Report of the Directors, to declare the amount of Dividend, and to elect three Directors in the room of

The Hon. W. PORTER, Esq.,
J. H. HOFMEYR, Esq., and
R. C. LOGIE, Esq.,

who retire in pursuance of the 24th Section of the Trust Deed.

By order of the Board,
TOBIAS MOSTERT, Cashier.

Cape Commercial Bank, Cape Town,
31st May, 1860.

WITH reference to the above Advertisement, Notice is hereby given that

The Hon. W. PORTER, Esq.,
J. H. HOFMEYR, Esq., and
R. C. LOGIE, Esq.

have been put in nomination to fill the above vacancies in the Direction of this Bank.

By order of the Board,
TOBIAS MOSTERT, Cashier.

Cape Commercial Bank,
14th June, 1860.

EQUITABLE

Marine Assurance Company.

NOTICE TO SHAREHOLDERS.

NOTICE is hereby given, in pursuance of the 22nd Section of the Trust Deed, that the Eleventh Annual General Meeting of Shareholders will be held at the Office of the Company, No. 6, Adderley-street, on

Monday, the 16th day of July,

when a statement of the Affairs and Business will be submitted, made up to the 30th day of June, 1860, also for the election of three Directors—who retire by rotation, and two Auditors,

The Directors who retire are the Hon. JOSEPH BARRY, Esq., M.L.C.; J. S. PRINCE, Esq., M.L.A.; and LOUIS GOLDMAN, Esq.,; and DANIEL MILLS and J. R. MARQUARD, Esq., as Auditors, but who are eligible for re-election.

The Chair to be taken at Eleven o'clock precisely

By order of the Board,
H. GORDON, Secretary.

Cape Town, 27th June, 1860.

Holloway's Pills.—These Pills are more efficacious in strengthening a debilitated constitution than any other medicine in the world. Persons of a nervous habit of body, and all who are suffering from week digestive organs, and whose health has become deranged by bilious affection, disordered stomach, or liver complaints, should lose no time in giving these admirable pills a fair trial. Coughs, colds, asthma, or shortness of breath, are also within the range of the sanative powers of this very remarkable medicine. The cures effected by these pills are not superficial or temporary, but complete and permanent. They are as mild as they are efficacious, and may be given with confidence to delicate females and young children.

OF CONSIDERABLE interest are the journals written during the long voyages to or from South Africa. One such, the diary kept by William and John Runciman, describes vividly the hardships and humour experienced during their three-month voyage from the Clyde to Port Natal (Durban) aboard the sailing ship *Olympia* in 1862. The following are extracts from this diary*:

April 15:
Last night some waves washed over the quarter deck and the seams not being very tight, both our beds got wet on one end, John's so badly that he turned out and lay on the sofa all night which he found cold and comfortless. We are both very squeamish but thankful we are no worse. We have scarcely been actually sick. Poor Mrs Boyd is suffering dreadfully, also her daughters. . . Every now and then we hear small imitations of Vesuvius during an eruption going on in her cabin which you may be sure does not tend to increase our appetite. . .

April 18:
. . . Today we got a considerable variety [*for dinner*]. Of course when our fresh provisions are finished, we will have more sameness. In a month or so, I will again describe our fare when we are on salt junk. The livestock on board consists of some 5 dozen fowls and 3 pigs.

April 20: 41°N 13°10′W
This morning we were lying in our berths when we suddenly heard the Captain call out, 'The foretopmast is gone! Call the Mate! All hands on deck!' and presently ensued a tremendous confusion. . . This, though not a serious disaster, is unfortunate as it compels us to shorten sail considerably. . . A schooner passed us today about noon. The Captain showed his number and bawled through his speaking trumpet, 'Report me!' Everything is in confusion on deck and as we are a little squeamish today, I think there will be no Prayers.

April 24: 37°59′N 11°30′W
. . . The programme of my days' proceedings at present is something like this – Waken at 8 – Breakfast at 9 – Lie in bed and read some book such as Colenso's 'Ten Weeks in Natal' or one of Waverleys till 11½ – Rise and go

*Reproduced with permission from the Natal Archival Depot (A 925)

Public Sale, at Mossel Bay,
OF THE
CONDEMNED SHIP 'ARGYLE,'
E. SMITH, COMMANDER,
ON FRIDAY, THE 10TH AUGUST NEXT.

THE UNDERSIGNED, as Agents of Captain E. SMITH, will cause to be sold as above, for account of whom it may concern, the HULL of the above Vessel, as she now lies in Mossel Bay, together with her TACKLE, APPAREL, ANCHORS and CABLES, SPARS, MASTS, SAILS, BOATS, STORES, &c., &c.

At same time and place will be sold, for account of whom it may concern, about

1,000 Bags Linseed and
100 Bales Cotton,

all more or less damaged by Sea Water, and landed from the above Vessel.

COLLISON, SHEPHERD, & Co., Agents.

Mossel Bay, 21st July, 1860.

J. VINTCENT, Auctioneer.

on deck at 12 – Promenade on deck till 2 – Dine till 2½ – Go on deck again, play draughts with Captain Jopp who can beat me, or chess with Mr Boyd and read a little till 5 – Go down to the cabin and play the fiddle till 6 – Take tea at 6 – Write diary, have a little conversation and sometimes take a toddy till 8½ – Go to bed. . . We are very pleased with Captain Jopp. . . I think he is a really good man too. Every night he reads his Bible for about an hour before going to bed. . . The mates too are, I think, respectable; we have never once heard anything in the shape of an oath. The strongest expressions the Captain ever uses, even when much excited, are 'Ah – Ah – Stupid!' or 'Oh you booby!'

May 4: 28° 16′N 7°31′W
From 2 o'clock this morning we were becalmed till about noon. Indeed for a fortnight the weather has been very baffling, now a contrary wind, now a calm, and now a squall, but scarcely ever a fair wind. . . A steamer has been keeping us company all day. . . She is under canvas and is supposed to be the *Rattler,* a tugboat going to Calcutta and which left the Clyde a short time before us. . .

June 11: 28° 39′S 33°48′W
When we went on deck this morning, a large full-rigged ship was to windward of us, about 5 miles distant. [*This was the* Hallard, *a vessel of about 1 200 tons which was 58 days out of Cardiff, bound for Hong Kong. At this stage the* Olympia *was 62 days out from Glasgow.*]

June 13: 32° 43′S 32°15′W
. . .A number of Cape pigeons and Cape hens have been following the ship for a day or two. . .

June 17: 35° 26′S 21°10′W
. . . We had the pleasure of tasting fresh pork at dinner but the recollection of seeing its honest face on deck the day before wasn't pleasant. . . We are now preparing for dirty weather. We had the mizzen topmast lowered and took in a reef of the main sail today. . .

June 21: 36°33′S 8°44′W
This is the shortest day – but quite long enough for us. . . There is a heavy sea running today and a strong wind. Every stitch of canvas is taken in, with the exception of the foresail, foretopsail and one staysail but the breeze is so strong that we are rushing and staggering along at a rate of 9 knots through waves from 20 to 25 feet high. . .

July 12: [*The final day of the diary and only a few nautical miles off Port Natal.*]
. . . Of the 12 days since we passed the Cape, the wind has been against us on six. The last pig has been killed and it is quite equal to the former two. . . We have plenty of water and are still living entirely on fresh and preserved [*sic*] provisions except at breakfast when we are regaled with ham, hardfish, herring, sardines, etc. – all excellent.

[*William Runciman died soon after arriving in Natal; his health, particularly what seems to have been a chest ailment, is referred to frequently in the diary. John Runciman, a young bachelor on arrival in Port Natal, later married Emmaline Buchanan and became a distinguished citizen of Pietermaritzburg.*]

2

1

Mayhew, Fisher, Byles, Trayner, Page, Oakley, and, more recently, Lloyd and Thomson – were known to many, and changes in command aroused great interest. Because so many South Africans travelled on these ships, either to and from England or on the very popular coastal passage between Cape Town and Durban, the mailships and their smaller 'intermediate' consorts were an integral part of the South African maritime scene ■

1 The Union liner *Scot,* photographed at the Loch Jetty in Table Bay harbour before her lengthening in 1896. In 1893 she had established a record time for the passage from England (14 days, 8 hours, 57 minutes), a record which stood until 1936 when the *Stirling Castle* reduced the time to 13 days, 9 hours. In later years, the mailships did the run in 11½ days.

AS STEAM REPLACED SAIL, services between England and South Africa became faster and more regular. The formation of the Union-Castle Line in 1900 was an important event in the maritime history of South Africa. The mailships, whose passenger complement in later years exceeded 700, became household names. New ships were greeted by crowds and were given massive press coverage. The mailship captains – men like Armstrong, Day, Baron, Brown,

2 The *Scot* after her lengthening. Because of her reputation for speed she was a good advert for the Union Line which, at that stage, was competing against the ships of Donald Currie's Castle Line for the contract to carry mail between England and South Africa. The main rival to the *Scot* was the *Dunottar Castle*. Both vessels, particularly the *Scot*, proved to be expensive to operate and were sold within a few years of the amalgamation of the Union Line and the Castle Line.

3 The *Adolf Woermann,* one of Deutsche Ost-Afrika Linie's ships which entered the African service after the First World War to replace vessels lost during the war. She continued the prestigious service to Germany until late in 1939. A fortnight after the outbreak of the Second World War she left Lobito in Angola and, in an attempt to reach Brazil undetected, was disguised at sea as the Portuguese liner *Nyassa*. The British armed merchant cruiser *Waimerama* spotted her and alerted the cruiser *Neptune*. To prevent her capture the *Adolf Woermann* was scuttled by her crew, all of whom were taken aboard the cruiser.

4 The Union-Castle intermediate liner *Llandovery Castle*, built in 1914. She did only two voyages between England and South Africa via Suez before the outbreak of the First World War, after which she was put onto the mail run for a year. She was eventually pressed into service by the Admiralty, first as a transport and later as a hospital ship. A few months before the end of the war she was torpedoed and sank with the loss of 234 people, an action which led to the prosecution of the senior officers of the offending submarine.

Her sister ship, the *Llanstephan Castle,* survived both World Wars, including a spell in the North Atlantic convoys, returned to the round-

Africa service of the Union-Castle Line in 1947, and was eventually withdrawn in 1952.

A later *Llandovery Castle* came out in 1926, did service in the Second World War and was scrapped in 1952.

5 From 1900 the Deutsche Ost-Afrika Linie used the *Kronprinz* on their round-Africa service, during which she and her stable-mates called at Dar es Salaam in German East Africa, at all South African ports, and at ports in West Africa. The service was later extended to include Lüderitzbucht and Swakopmund in South West Africa. At the outbreak of the First World War, she was in Lourenço Marques (Maputo) and remained there for two years until she was taken over by the Portuguese, who operated her as the *Quelimane.*

England-South Africa-Australia service. She and her consorts later came under the control of Shaw Savill, who had also operated a passenger/cargo service to Australia for many years. She was the last word in passenger ships at the time, and was the largest regular liner to call here until the arrival of the *Arundel Castle* in 1921. In 1940 she collided with Bank Line's *Testbank* off the West Coast while both ships were blacked out. The *Testbank,* badly damaged and down by the bow, made it to Cape Town, while the *Ceramic,* escorted by a tug and a

1 The 'basket', in which passengers were lowered to a tug to be taken ashore, was in use at East London and Port Elizabeth until the 1930s. It was also used at Mossel Bay, and even at Port Nolloth in the early years. Inclement weather frequently prevented the use of the basket and passengers had to disembark at the next port of call.
2 The *Ceramic,* a White Star liner built in 1913 for the

cruiser, went to Walvis Bay for temporary repairs. Two years later the *Ceramic* was torpedoed in the Atlantic off the North African coast and went down quickly. Over 600 lives were lost; the sole survivor was rescued by the attacking submarine.
3 The *Stella Polaris,* a superb Norwegian cruise ship, seen here in Table Bay in 1936. She had been built nine years previously and had a long life, trading until the late 1960s.

4 The *Windhuk* and her sister ship, the *Pretoria,* were the largest Deutsche Ost-Afrika Linie passenger ships on the Germany-South Africa run from

1937. They were also the last on that service. (Note the Swastika flag at the stern.) Both ships ended the war in Allied hands. The *Windhuk* was seized by Brazil and sold to the United States Navy, which scrapped her in 1966. The *Pretoria* was in Germany when war broke out and she remained there to be captured by Allied forces in 1945. Thereafter, as the *Empire Doon* and later the *Empire Orwell,* she transported British troops and other personnel until she was sold for service as a pilgrim ship between Indonesia and Jiddah. **5** The *City of London,* a tip-top Ellerman and Bucknall liner, photographed at Port Elizabeth. The excellence of the cuisine and service aboard these ships and their successors made them very popular. This vessel, built in Belfast yards in 1907, saw service in both World Wars before being scrapped in 1946.

ELLERMAN AND BUCKNALL, Shaw Savill, Bullard King and other shipping lines also plied the England-South Africa route for many years, and until the Second World War the Deutsche Ost-Afrika Linie provided a regular service. Between the wars a number of first-rate Italian liners challenged the mailships for speed, and from Lisbon came vessels which linked Portugal with her colonies in West and East Africa. Yet another coastal and foreign service available to South African travellers was provided by the smart vessels of the Holland-Afrika Lijn. The panelled interiors and comfortable cabins of the *-fontein* ships were talked about long after a voyage had ended. From 1938 a service to the Far East and South America was provided by another Dutch concern, Royal Interocean Lines, in their three triple-screw ships, the *Ruys,* the *Boissevain* and the *Tegelberg.* And between the wars, Japanese passenger ships called regularly at South African ports ∎

2

THE ARUNDEL CASTLE
Nearly Forty Years on the
Mailship Service

Launched in Belfast in 1921, the
Arundel Castle was a favourite
with South African voyagers. It
was said that her four funnels
implied speed and associated her
with the North Atlantic liners,
though most of these were larger
and faster than anything on the
South African run. Her arrival in
Cape Town heralded an era of
larger ships on the South African
service and caused more

excitement and public interest
than was usually the case with
new mailships, probably because
she was the first four-funneller
on a regular schedule to South
Africa.

In order to provide a faster
mail service she returned to her
builders' yards in 1937, was re-
engined and lengthened, and
came back as a two-funneller
with oil-fired turbines and a
clipper bow. She served as a
troopship during the Second
World War, after which she
returned to the mail run and
remained on it until 1958. It was
a day of great nostalgia when she
left Table Bay harbour's A Berth
for the last time in December of
that year. The rousing farewell
given to the last two-funnelled
mailship included a convoy of all
the harbour's tugs, dressed
overall for the occasion.

This was the first of many last-
voyage departures for the
mailships in post-war years, a
trend which continued until the
last Union-Castle liner left
South Africa in 1977 ∎

1 The second *Arundel Castle*,
built in 1895 and sold to Danish
owners in 1905, was typical of
the Cape liners of the time. Sail
assisted her coal-fired engines
when necessary. An earlier
Arundel Castle was a sailing ship

1

4

which traded to the East from 1864 to 1883.

2 The third *Arundel Castle,* alongside East Pier in Table Bay harbour. Until the mid-1930s, when the Duncan Dock took shape, East Pier was the departure wharf for the northbound mailship. This photograph probably depicts the vessel during her maiden voyage.

3 The only four-funnellers on the South African service pass each other in Table Bay harbour. The

Arundel Castle is coaling for the northbound voyage to Southampton, while the *Windsor Castle* is outward bound for the coast. Coaling was a tedious and time-consuming operation. The side of the ship was partially covered with canvas to prevent coaldust from entering the accommodation. In earlier years each sack of coal was carried aboard and emptied through chutes into the ship's bunker spaces. Later this operation was streamlined a little, but the dust

problem remained. Some of the early mailships (and most other coal-fired steamships) carried sacks of coal on top of the cargo in their holds so that bunkers could be replenished at sea during the long voyages. The conversion of both of the four-funnellers to oil-fired steam turbines just before the Second World War removed the problems of coaling and increased the operational efficiency of the ships.

4 The *Windsor Castle* after her refit in 1937. At the outbreak of war she was commissioned for service by the Admiralty. While carrying troops in the Mediterranean in 1943 she was attacked by aircraft and began to sink. Salvage attempts were in vain and she foundered.

5 The *Windsor Castle,* as she was before her refit, undocks in Table Bay harbour. She came into service a year after her sister ship, the *Arundel Castle.* Each ship had accommodation for first- and tourist-class passengers. In their earlier years both ships had straight stems and cruiser sterns, the latter being a departure from the customary counter stern of previous Union-Castle vessels. They also differed from previous vessels in having two tiers of lifeboats.

5

1

UNION-CASTLE LINE had
offices in all the major
ports, and agents almost
everywhere in South Africa.
Even in some of the more remote
towns there were posters
advertising a leisurely sea
voyage to England ('the sunshine
way'), as well as coastal trips. In
the early days at Kimberley the
Union-Castle flag was hoisted to
herald the safe arrival of the
mailship in Table Bay harbour,
after which the inhabitants of
the diamond-fields eagerly
looked forward to the arrival of
the mail train from Cape Town.

Waiting on the wharf for each
mailship would be the 'boat
train', which conveyed transit
passengers from Cape Town to
Johannesburg and the former
Rhodesias. For the northbound
voyage, passengers from the
interior were taken direct to

Table Bay harbour's mailship
wharf by train. Eventually, alas,
the boat train was discontinued.

Even booking your ticket used
to be an exciting affair. On
entering the Union-Castle office
you would be ushered to the desk
of one of the many booking
clerks. 'Yes sir, we have a
comfortable port-side cabin for
you on the *Stirling,* and you can
return from Southampton on the
Athlone, leaving England during
the first week of November.' The
ticket was a huge folder which
included your baggage labels. A
week or so before sailing you
would go to the office to get your
cabin number: 'Yes sir, number
C240. I'm sure you will enjoy the
trip. . .' Most of these clerks were
retrenched when things became
tight in the early 1960s, and
booking subsequently became a
rather impersonal experience ■

1 Three mailships, the
Winchester Castle (shown here),
the *Carnarvon Castle* and the
Warwick Castle, entered the
South African service between
1926 and 1931. They were of
similar design and were the first
mailships to be powered by diesel
engines. All underwent a major
refit in the late 1930s, during
which they were re-engined and
their two funnels were replaced
by one. The *Warwick Castle* was
torpedoed and lost in November
1942. The *Winchester Castle* was
involved, *inter alia,* in the
Madagascan Campaign, and
returned to the mail service after
the war. In 1960 she was
withdrawn and replaced by the
Windsor Castle.

The tug shown here, the
Ludwig Wiener, was a dual-
purpose harbour and salvage
vessel, which dragged many

2

3

4

ships from the rocks, hauled sailing vessels out to sea to pick up the trade winds or the tail of the Roaring Forties, and held hundreds of ships in the teeth of a south-east gale. Her later years were spent in service at Durban harbour.

2 The *Durham Castle* (shown here) and her two sisters, the *Dover Castle* and the *Dunluce Castle,* were intermediate liners which came out in 1904. The *Dover Castle* was sunk during the First World War; the *Dunluce Castle* survived both wars and was scrapped in 1945; the *Durham Castle* was sold in 1939 but was reprieved at the start of the war. She lasted only a few months, being sunk early in 1940 off the Scottish coast.

3 An excellent view of the *Balmoral Castle* leaving Cape Town. Until the late 1930s, there were four two-funnelled mail steamers on the run: the *Armadale Castle,* the *Kenilworth Castle,* the *Edinburgh Castle* and this vessel. The requirements of a faster mail service brought their careers to an end, and all except the *Edinburgh Castle* were scrapped before the Second World War.

4 The *Llangibby Castle,* the last two-funnelled intermediate liner. Her war years as a trooper had a few dramatic moments, particularly the occasion when a torpedo ripped a hole in her stern, damaging her rudder. However, she survived the war to return to the round-Africa service for another nine years before making way for vessels of the *Rhodesia Castle*-class in the early 1950s.

1 Built in 1939 as the *Pretoria Castle,* this vessel was converted to an aircraft carrier during the war. On her return to the merchant service, she was renamed *Warwick Castle,* taking the name of the mailship which had been lost in 1942.

The *Warwick Castle* and her sister ship, the *Durban Castle,* were joined on the round-Africa haul in the early 1950s by the slightly smaller *Rhodesia Castle, Kenya Castle* and *Braemar Castle.* Some of these ships went from South Africa to London via Suez, and others sailed in the opposite direction. The *Bloemfontein Castle,* a one-class, single-masted intermediate liner, covered the London-South Africa-Beira route during the 1950s.

After the British colonies in East and West Africa had gained independence, and with the introduction of regular air services, Union-Castle links to these areas were curtailed and eventually ceased in the 1960s.

2 Shaw Savill's magnificently unique *Dominion Monarch* which, apart from a seven-year break for wartime trooping and refitting, plied the England-New Zealand route via South Africa and Australia from 1938. Her public rooms were exquisitely decorated, the lounge having Canadian elm panelling made from pilings taken from the base of Waterloo Bridge in London. A one-class ship with a large amount of deck space, she was extremely popular. However, the four-week voyage to Australasia could not compete with the advantages offered by the airlines and she was withdrawn

from service in 1962 to make way for the round-the-world liner *Northern Star*.
3 The two-funnelled *Carnarvon Castle*.
4 The *Carnarvon Castle* leaving Table Bay harbour in 1962 on her last voyage.

THE CARNARVON CASTLE
Armed Merchant Cruiser, Troopship and Mailship

The *Carnarvon Castle* came into service in 1926 and was the first motor-ship on the mail run. She was also the largest vessel in the fleet until the arrival of the *Stirling Castle* in 1936. Late in the following year she underwent a major refit which altered her profile considerably: her two funnels were replaced by one and she was given a clipper bow.

At the outbreak of the Second World War she was southbound, a week out of Cape Town. On arrival there her coastal passengers were disembarked and, requisitioned by the Admiralty, she sailed round to Simonstown to be fitted out as an armed merchant cruiser with 150-mm guns, her main armament. Deployed on the South Atlantic Station, she moved out towards South America to attempt to curtail the activities of German surface raiders in the area. Probably her most famous (though unsuccessful) encounter was her engagement with the German raider *Thor* in December 1940. During the brief action (about 1½ hours) the *Carnarvon Castle* was hit several times and much of her electrical gunnery control equipment was put out of action. Despite claims to the contrary, the *Thor* appears to have escaped without damage.

The mailship also saw action in Operation Bellringer off the South African coast in 1941, during which a number of Vichy-French ships were captured while trying to return to France from Madagascar. From 1943 she patrolled the Atlantic Narrows to intercept blockade runners, but as the days of armed merchant cruisers were running out, she sailed to New York for conversion to a troopship. As such she did duty in the Mediterranean and the Indian Ocean. After hostilities had ceased, she was used to repatriate South African and Rhodesian troops.

On her return to the Union-Castle Line she was initially fitted out as an immigrant ship with over 1 000 berths, but in 1949, with the post-war immigration rush over, she reverted to her normal complement of 160 first-class and 450 tourist-class passengers.

In 1962 she left Table Bay harbour for the last time, to be replaced by the *Transvaal Castle*, later renamed the *S.A. Vaal* ∎

ONE ROSE EARLY to be at the quayside before daybreak to meet the ship. There she was, just off the breakwater, at dead-slow ahead while the pilot boarded her. One tug went out into the roadstead, the other waited inside the harbour. The early morning glow did something magical to those mailships, with their lavender hulls and white superstructure. As the ship came nearer, one could identify Uncle or Aunt, Granny or Cousin John. The first lines went ashore, the gangway was set in place, and an hour or two later, with customs and immigration formalities completed, relatives and friends were reunited.

Nostalgia probably grips us most when we remember the departure from Table Bay harbour each Friday. What precision! What atmosphere! Friends and relatives crowded into the cabin (the children playing with the punka louvre ventilator!) after lunch had been enjoyed in the saloon or tea in the lounge. Then the ship's bell, followed by the broadcast: 'This ship is due to sail shortly. Will all those not travelling aboard please make their way ashore.' The streamers, the tears, the waving friends below. Finally the pilot arrived, his flag was run up, tugs came alongside and the berthing gangs appeared on the wharfside. At the stroke of 4 o'clock the last line was slipped, the Blue Peter was lowered, the towing hawser from the tug became taut and, with the throb of her engines hard astern, the liner moved away from the quay. Streamers snapped as final farewells were called. Then half-ahead, past the bullnose she went, foghorn blaring, tugs screeching. The pilot, photographed by many for their holiday albums, disembarked into the smoky pilot-tug below.

Beyond the breakwater, as Table Mountain dropped astern, the 'Cape rollers' heaved the ship while her passengers dressed for dinner, which might consist of turtle soup, followed by grilled Yarmouth sole, roast beef and Yorkshire pudding, and peach Melba. While having a quiet cup of coffee in the lounge one looked ahead to days of relaxation in the tropical sun, and to magical evenings filled with fun and frivolity.

After each evening's entertainment – a dance, a film show, or perhaps a fancy dress ball – one took the evening air on deck and then returned to the cabin to find the bunk prepared and the bulkhead light on. With the gentle rolling and creaking of the ship as she took the sea, sleep seemed to come so easily.

Up bright and early each morning for a full English breakfast, followed by swimming, a game of deck-quoits, reading . . . Before long it was time for lunch, and then for afternoon tea. The Bay of Biscay often had something in store, but when all was said and done, only wonderful memories of a sea voyage remained ∎

1 Dawn arrival aboard the *S.A. Vaal*. Table Bay harbour's container basin mirrors the sky.

3

4

5

2 Aboard the *Arundel Castle*. Even in her later years, the occasional pall of smoke was visible for miles.
3 Usually two South African harbour tugs were needed to move the mailships. In undocking procedures, one tug was attached to swing the bow; the other towed the stern away from the wharf, as depicted here. The old steam tugs had a manila towing spring to which a steel hawser was attached for the tow. Each port seemed to have its problems for the liners. Wind delayed the ships on many occasions, particularly at Cape Town, Port Elizabeth and East London. There were times when the call at East London was abandoned because of the gales sweeping up the Buffalo River, as happened on the last voyage of the *S.A. Oranje*. Pilots there also had to contend with the small

turning basin and the river currents. Durban's shifting sandbars occasionally brought a liner to a halt.
4 Past the bullnose at Table Bay harbour. This photograph from the *Carnarvon Castle* in the late 1950s shows the Second World War harbour defence structures, since demolished. It is clear that the Cape Doctor was blowing that day!
5 Crossing the Line, the keenly awaited or feared ceremony involving passengers who had never crossed the Equator by sea. 'King Neptune' and his men initiated the brave to the delight of the more seasoned (or wiser) travellers. This ceremony was one of the entertainments which featured in the elaborate programme of events aboard passenger ships. On the final night aboard there was usually a splendid gala banquet.

1 Deck games aboard a mailship in 1958.
2 Gangway for passengers boarding the *S.A. Oranje*.
3 Renamed in 1966, Safmarine's *S.A. Oranje* was launched as the *Pretoria Castle* in 1947 by Mrs Smuts, the wife of the South African Prime Minister, Field Marshal Smuts. The occasion was unusual in that Mrs Smuts was not present at the launching but pressed a button installed in her home near Pretoria whereby landline and radio transmissions were activated to release a bottle of wine which smashed against the ship's bow at the launching slipway in Belfast. It was also the only occasion that a mailship was launched with the traditional wording in Afrikaans. It was perhaps symbolic of her later career as a South African-registered mailship that the *Pretoria Castle* flew the South African flag from her jackstaff as she moved down the slipway.

She was the first post-war Union-Castle mailship to enter service, followed a year later by her sister ship, the *Edinburgh Castle*. Both were replacements

for war losses. The other three post-war mailships, the *Pendennis Castle* (1959), the *Windsor Castle* (1960) and the *Transvaal Castle* (1961), replaced obsolete vessels.

Because of Safmarine's active involvement in the mailship service, they took over the *Pretoria Castle* and the *Transvaal Castle* (which they renamed the *S.A. Vaal*) in 1966.

The photograph shows the *S.A. Oranje* leaving Cape Town for the last time in 1975. She did the coastal passage to Durban before crossing to the shipbreakers' yards in Taiwan.

4 Safmarine's former flagship, the *S.A. Vaal*, off the Cape Peninsula. Launched in 1961 as the *Transvaal Castle*, she was Union-Castle's 'hotel ship', providing an interesting departure from the strictly-applied class divisions on other mailships. After being taken over by Safmarine her name was changed at an impressive ceremony in Cape Town, and in 1969 the State President, Mr J.J. Fouché, officiated at her flag-changing. She was withdrawn from the mail service in 1977 and

now cruises, mainly in the Caribbean, as the *Festivale*.

5 Commodore Robin Thomson, the first Safmarine officer to command a mailship (the *S.A. Oranje*). He was later promoted and took over the *S.A. Vaal* from Commodore Norman Lloyd, a Union-Castle officer who had begun his maritime career on the South African training ship *General Botha*. Commodore Thomson is also a 'Bothie Boy', having served on the training ship just before the Second World War.

The first ship on which he served, the Blue Funnel liner *Anchises,* was sunk by enemy action shortly after he joined her, and the young Apprentice Thomson spent two days in a open lifeboat in the North Atlantic before being rescued.

He joined Safmarine in 1947 as Second Mate on the *Vergelegen*. Promoted to Master of one of their freighters in the early 1950s, he commanded most of the company's vessels at one time or another. His appointment as Staff Captain, Mailship Captain and finally Commodore brought his fine career to a pinnacle.

After the demise of the mailships he flew his Fleet Commodore's flag in the *S.A. Helderberg,* one of Safmarine's large container ships, until his retirement in 1983.

His expertise was again required in 1984 during the maiden voyage of the *Astor*, Safmarine's new liner, when he was called upon to command the vessel.

1 On the British India Line's service between India and East Africa, the *Karanja* called frequently at Durban and occasionally at Cape Town. When she was withdrawn in 1976, the sea passenger service between South Africa and India came to an end.

2 Streamers at the departure of the *Empress of England,* which did a number of cruises to South America in the early 1960s on charter to a travel organization. Her sister ship, the *Empress of Britain,* and the former Pacific Steam Navigation Company liner *Reina del Mar,* also cruised from South African ports.

3 Ellerman and Bucknall's *City of Durban* which, with three sister ships – *City of Port Elizabeth, City of Exeter* and *City of York* – operated a passenger and cargo service from London to ports in South Africa and

Mozambique. All four vessels were sold in 1971 for service in the Mediterranean Sea, their places on the Southern African service being taken by cargo ships.

4 The spoon-bowed *Jagersfontein* operated Holland-Afrika Lijn's service to Southern Africa from 1934 until taken over for wartime duties, during which she was sunk in the North Atlantic in 1942. A second *Jagersfontein* came onto the run in 1950 (she had actually been laid down before the war and had been given two other names before her final one) to join her sister ship, the *Oranjefontein*. Another sister ship, the *Klipfontein*, sank off the coast of Mozambique in 1953 after hitting uncharted rocks. The *Oranjefontein* and the *Jagersfontein* were scrapped in 1967.

5 The Portuguese liners *Imperio* (shown here), *Patria*, and *Infante Dom Henrique*, and their rivals the *Angola*, the *Moçambique* and the *Principe Perfeito*, linked Portugal to her African provinces of Angola and Mozambique. By the mid-1970s these ships had all been withdrawn.

6 Holland-Afrika Lijn's smart passenger ship *Randfontein*, which first came out to South Africa in 1958. In 1971, after the Europe-South Africa passenger trade had dried up, she was taken over by other Dutch interests in the Far East.

7 Built in 1931, the *Tjisadane* plied the Far East-South Africa-South America trade for Royal Interocean Lines during the postwar period. Probably her most notable achievement was her involvement in the rescue of the Tristan da Cunha islanders during the volcanic eruption in 1961. She was scrapped in 1962 and replaced by fast cargo ships.

1 A fine study of the fast Italian liner *Duilio,* which came this way between the wars. She and her sister ship, the *Giulio Cesare,* were victims of the Second World War.

2 The *Medic,* one of three sister ships on White Star Line's run from Britain to Australia via South Africa. Immigrants to Australia could travel cheaply on these ships. At the beginning of the Anglo-Boer War all three, still new ships, were requisitioned as transports. The

Medic survived the First World War and was sold to whaling interests, who converted her into a factory ship with a stern slipway.

3 The Italian liner *Africa,* and her sister ship, the *Europa,* were launched after the Second World War and offered an attractive East Coast service to Italy until the closure of the Suez Canal in 1967. Smaller than their predecessors, the *Duilio* and the *Giulio Cesare,* they were nevertheless popular,

particularly for the leg via Suez. High operating costs and the looming container era swept these vessels aside. Now two container ships on the South Africa-Genoa haul bear these names.

4 When Shaw Savill's *Southern Cross* began their round-the-world service (England-South Africa-Australasia-Panama-England) in 1955, she was the first large passenger-ship with the funnel aft. Her facilities were the epitome of luxury, but were functional at the same time. Many South Africans will remember those exotic ports of call: Fiji, Tahiti, Panama, Barbados, and more. But having no cargo spaces to offset increasing losses, she and her sister ship, the *Northern Star,* were withdrawn. The *Southern Cross* was sold to cruise operators who renamed her *Calypso* (shown here). The *Northern Star* went to the shipbreakers' yards in 1975. Thus ended the centuries-old passenger link with Australasia.

5 The Blue Funnel liner *Ixion,* one of four similar vessels, was on the Australian run after the Second World War. These ships were switched to the Suez/Panama route in the 1950s but were seen here again during the Suez closures. All four ships of this class were scrapped in 1972.

6 For those South Africans wishing to take a sea voyage to New York, Farrell Lines had the war-built steamers *African Enterprise* (shown here) and

African Endeavor. These ships could seldom have paid their way, and in the face of improving air services both vessels ceased to call at South African ports.

ALTHOUGH THE SECOND World War changed the pattern of the passenger trade (the cessation of German and Japanese services to South Africa is an example), several factors in combination were responsible for the reduction and eventual elimination of the post-war passenger fleets on the South African run. In the space of twenty years more than forty ships were withdrawn and no replacements were ordered.

Air travel had become more sophisticated, was obviously faster, and eventually became cheaper than ocean travel. The independence of many African countries, particularly during the late 1950s and early 1960s, reduced the flow of expatriates from Europe and thereby also the number of potential passengers. This led to the withdrawal of many of the liners on the various African hauls, the Union-Castle intermediates being among those which disappeared.

Because of high fuel prices and the high wages paid to European seamen, passenger ships, with their large crews and heavy fuel consumption, became too expensive to operate. The advent of containerization was the final blow for passenger ships because they had no space to carry containers. Thus, regular passenger services to South Africa ceased completely in the 1970s. Only the occasional call by cruise liners provided an opportunity for sea travel, but the high fares for berths on these vessels prevented the average South African from taking to the sea again ■

DESPITE the disappearance of regular passenger liners, the mailship service was resumed in a rather different form when the small cargo/passenger ship, the *St Helena,* began a service between England and the islands of St Helena and Ascension. Because such a high proportion of the supplies for the islands come from South Africa, and because many South Africans have relatives on St Helena, the service was extended to Cape Town. When the *St Helena* was requisitioned for service during the Falklands War, an even

smaller vessel came on the run. Soon thereafter a former Blue Funnel liner, the *Centaur,* took over, but her cargo spaces were seldom full and she always had many empty berths. The *St Helena* resumed the service on her release by the Admiralty after the war, and the *Centaur* returned to her original trade in the Far East.

A German cruise liner, the *Astor,* put into South African ports during December 1983 and proved to be a foretaste of things to come. She had been bought by South Africa's premier shipping line, Safmarine, to operate a point-to-point service between South Africa and Southampton. Occasional cruises to Indian Ocean islands and South America would form part of her schedule during the off-season for northbound voyages.

She was refitted in West German yards and made her maiden voyage in Safmarine colours during April 1984. The passenger service between England and South Africa, with its former atmosphere and trappings, was resumed. Even the boat train from Johannesburg made a reappearance.

The new concept of passenger ship operation, whereby point-to-point sailings are combined with cruising, should be very different, because the operators have a more flexible schedule and advantage can be taken of optimum passenger demand on any route. In any event, a South African passenger ship does provide a new dimension to the merchant fleet ■

1 The *Astor* in her colours as a German cruise liner.
2 The *Astor* arriving in Table Bay harbour after her first southbound voyage in Safmarine colours.

1 The glorious Cunard liner *Caronia,* the doyen of post-war cruise ships, first called at Cape Town in 1950 and thereafter became a regular visitor to this country. Her arrival brought hundreds of wealthy Americans to South Africa, and also thousands of sightseers to the harbours. But as fuel prices and portage bills rocketed in the 1960s, she was sold to Panamanian operators. She then experienced one problem after another and finally came to an ignominious end: as the *Caribia* she was wrecked on Guam Island while under tow to Taiwanese breakers.

2 The *Sagafjord,* built for the Norwegian American Line in 1965, has undergone a considerable refit to maintain her position among the best of the world's cruise liners. The cruise programme of her Norwegian owners took her inevitably into the fjords and to North Cape, as well as to the Arctic ice barrier. But her usual cruise areas were the Caribbean and Mediterranean. Occasional round-the-world cruises brought her and her consort, the *Vistafjord,* to South African ports. In 1984 she was seen in local waters in Cunard colours, having been bought by the British shipping group.

3 The *Queen Elizabeth 2,* Cunard's more fuel-efficient

replacement for the *Caronia,* has visited Cape Town and Durban a number of times. Like her predecessor, and indeed the *Franconia* before that, she has acquired a reputation for the utmost luxury – at the utmost prices. Also like her predecessor, she is stalked by spiralling

running costs which make it difficult for her owners to operate her profitably.

4 Longer than the *Queen Elizabeth* by about 1,5 metres, the *France,* seen here in Table Bay during a world cruise, is the

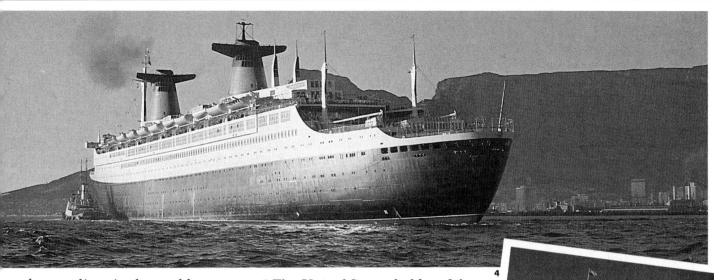

longest liner in the world. Shortly after this call she was laid up in Le Havre and was later sold to the Norwegians, who renamed her *Norway*. She has yet to visit South African ports in her new colours.

5 The pride of the Royal Mail Lines, the *Andes*, during a fleeting visit to Cape Town. Until the late 1950s she had operated a regular service between Britain and South America, but owing to the decline in that trade she switched to cruising. She was scrapped in 1971.

6 The *United States*, holder of the Blue Riband, visited this part of the world only once. In the course of that visit she used her turn of speed to set a new record for the passage between Port Elizabeth and Cape Town, leaving the former port early in the morning and arriving in Table Bay at about 21h00 that night. Although she steered a course well wide of land, the residents of the Atlantic suburbs of Cape Town clearly saw her brilliant illuminations as she raced towards the Table Bay pilot station.

CHAPTER
V
THE CARGO TRADE

THE FIRST REGULAR CARGO service to South Africa was inaugurated in 1851, when the 500-ton *Bosphorus* sailed from England to the Cape. Her owners, the General Screw Steam Ship Company, had been awarded the first mail contract. These early vessels were steamers but were also fully rigged to conserve coal when favourable sailing conditions prevailed.

After the demise of the General Screw Steam Ship Company, the Union Steam Ship Company took over the mail contract. Its first vessel on this run, the 526-ton *Dane,* arrived in October 1857 and was the forerunner of a service to South Africa that was terminated only when the last Union-Castle mailship left Table Bay harbour in 1977 ■

(Previous pages) Formerly a Finnish vessel, the barque *Lawhill* became a household name in South Africa. She was seized in East London when Finland was invaded by Russia during the Second World War and technically became an 'enemy' of South Africa. The Department of Customs and Excise requested the Railways and Harbours Administration to operate her as part of their fleet that normally traded to Australia to load jarrah railway sleepers. Many South Africans, including young men straight from the training ship *General Botha,* sailed in her. Because of competition from steam and the return of other Railway ships to their normal duties after the war, the *Lawhill* was sold to prospective operators. However, she was beached on the shores of

Delagoa Bay soon after her sale and was left there to rot.

This fine painting by marine artist Peter Bilas captures the drama of sail as the *Lawhill* ploughs her course along the South African coast.

1 Owned by the Hamburg-based Woermann Linie, the *Gertrud Woermann* was built in 1886 and was the first of four vessels to bear this name. The Woermann Linie had traded to West Africa since 1849, and in the 1880s and 1890s it extended its services to South West Africa and the Cape. The *Gertrud Woermann* arrived in 1900 to serve the ports between Swakopmund and Cape Town. She travelled at a modest 10 knots and could accommodate 30 passengers. Her end came when she was wrecked in thick fog near Port Nolloth in August 1903.

2 Registered in Drammen, Norway, the *South Africa* was built on the Clyde in 1909 and is pictured here in the Victoria Basin, Cape Town.

3 Built at the famous Blohm and Voss shipyard in Hamburg in 1922, the *Cassel* had four turbines geared to a single shaft. Her owners, the Deutsch-Australische-Dampfschiffahrtges., were operating a service to Australia via the Cape when they were absorbed by the Hamburg-Amerika Linie in 1926.

1 The *Trewidden* and other tramp steamers owned by the Hain Steam Ship Company were regularly seen in South African waters carrying mainly bulk cargoes such as coal, maize and sugar.

2 Shipping links between Portugal and Africa were established by the Portuguese Royal Mail Line (Mala Real Portugeza) in 1889 with the arrival of the passenger vessel *Rei De Portugal*. This monthly service was short-lived, however, since the company ceased to operate about four years later. A revival was inaugurated in November 1906 when the *Portugal* (shown here), owned by the Empreza Nacional de Nav. (ENN), began to call at Cape Town on her voyages to Mozambique. After the First World War the ENN was integrated into a new company, the Companhia Nacional de Nav., and in the following years a number of second-hand Belgian, Dutch and German liners were acquired, all of them carrying large numbers of passengers.

3 During the 1930s Union-Castle built six reefer ships to carry South African perishables to Britain and Europe. The *Rochester Castle* (shown here) and her slightly older near-sister ship the *Roslin Castle* were the only two of these vessels to survive the war. In 1942 the convoys to relieve Malta became progressively more perilous and many ships were sunk. In August of that year fourteen British merchantmen left Liverpool in convoy for Malta, only five of these reaching their destination. The *Rochester Castle* was the first to enter Valletta harbour, having survived almost continuous attacks by E-boats, dive bombers and submarines.

By 1947 all the war losses among Union-Castle fruit ships had been replaced.

4 The second *Umvoti*, formerly the *Comrie Castle*, was acquired by Bullard King in 1924. This company had for many years operated a direct service to Natal jointly with Rennies. However, in 1919 Lord Kylsant, the chairman of Union-Castle, was instrumental in Bullard King becoming a unit of the Kylsant Group. Some years later four Union-Castle ships, including the *Comrie Castle* and the *Cluny Castle,* were transferred to Bullard King. The tug shown in the photograph is the *Sir David Hunter*.

5 The *Clan Stuart* was one of about thirty vessels known as 'turret-deck' ships, built between 1897 and 1907 for Clan Line of Glasgow (see next page). They were unusual in their design, the hull taking an inward sweep about 1,5 metres above the water-line. This resulted in the deck being about half the width of the beam of the vessel, and was apparently done to save on Suez Canal dues. The *Clan Stuart,* built in 1900, came to grief in 1914 at Glencairn, near Simonstown, when she drifted ashore in a strong south-easter.

3

4

5

1

2

CAYZER, IRVINE AND
Company, with its Clan
Line ships, played an
increasingly important part in
the developing trade to South
Africa in the latter part of the
nineteenth century. As there was
no shipping link between
Scotland or the North of England
and the Cape, a service from the
Clyde and the Mersey was
started by Clan Line in 1881. At
the outbreak of the First World

War, Clan Line owned a fleet of
fifty-six ships, half of these being
lost and replaced during the war.

Over the years the company
has provided much-needed
refrigerated space for transporting South African fruit to
Britain and Europe. Another
specialized field has been the
handling of heavy-lift cargoes,
for which some vessels were
equipped with derricks capable
of lifting up to 165 tons ■

1 The *Clan Farquhar,* typical of
the Clan Line ships of the 1920s.
2 The *Clan Lamont,* completed in
1939. A large number of vessels
of this type were built and war
losses were heavy.
3 The *Clan Cumming,* completed
in 1946, was almost identical to
the pre-war vessels.
4 The *Clan Graham* was built in
1961 and belonged to a new class
of vessels, the first of which (the
Clan MacIver) arrived in South

5

6

3

4

Africa in 1958. They differed from previous Clan ships in that the superstructure was further aft, thus allowing four holds forward and one aft of the accommodation.

5 Harrison cargo ships have traded to the Cape and Natal since 1901. In 1911 the company acquired the complete fleet of Rennies of Aberdeen, and until 1921 they kept up the passenger service inherited from Rennies.

Since then they have concentrated on the cargo trade. Built in 1951, their 8 000-ton vessel the *Wanderer* typified the more modern motor-ships of the post-war period.

6 The *Custodian*, an example of Harrison's heavy-lift ships that visited South Africa more recently. Vessels of this type were easily distinguished by the Stülcken derrick amidships and the bridge structure very far

forward. Containerization and the subsequent rationalization of services saw the disappearance from South African waters of the distinctive Harrison funnel with its red and white bands. At present the company has a share with Ellermans (see next page) in the fully cellular vessel *City of Durban*.

7 An earlier *City of Durban*, built in 1921 and photographed at Liverpool.

7

1

ELLERMAN AND BUCKNALL'S association with South Africa began in the 1890s, when the company secured a lucrative contract for the transportation of railway material for the new line being built from the Witwatersrand to Delagoa Bay. Originally known as Bucknall Brothers, the company's first vessels to call at South African ports were the *Afrikander* and the *Kaffir*. There was a problem finding cargoes for homeward-bound ships, with the result that many of them crossed the Indian Ocean in ballast to load rice in Burma. Passengers were first carried in 1895, but regular cargo services always remained the company's main concern. At present Ellermans operate the container ship *City of Durban* in conjunction with Harrisons on the Europe-Southern Africa run ■

3

4

1 The *City of Johannesburg,* built for Ellerman Lines in 1947, was propelled by diesel engines, hence the shortness of her funnel.
2 The *City of Cape Town,* completed in 1959, originally traded to Australia as the *City of Melbourne.* She carried general and refrigerated cargo, and had the most powerful diesel engine built in the United Kingdom at the time: a twelve-cylinder turbo-charged Sulzer developing over 18 000 b.h.p.
3 The *City of Pretoria* was one of four sister ships completed in 1947. They were twin-screw turbine steamers and formed part of the rebuilding programme undertaken by most British shipping companies after the war.

4 The motor-ship *Forresbank* was owned by Andrew Weir and Company of London who first started trading to India and South Africa in 1906 with chartered tonnage. They later acquired three veterans from Bucknalls. The *Forresbank,* completed in 1925, was wrecked off the coast of Pondoland.
5 The *Grootekerk* was one of a larger number of steamers, known as 'Victory' ships, built in the United States to help the war effort. Many European liner companies replaced war losses with 'Victory' and 'Liberty' ships to enable them to resume disrupted services. The *Grootekerk* was taken over by the Holland-Afrika Lijn in 1946.

5

1

SHIPS FLYING THE AMERICAN flag first started calling at ports in Southern Africa after the First World War. During this period the United States Shipping Board operated cargo vessels and introduced a monthly service to Southern Africa in 1922. The ships were operated on behalf of the Shipping Board by Mallory Transport Lines Inc., popularly known as the American South Africa Line. In 1925 the fleet of five steamers was acquired by a private shipowner, and after the Second World War the American South Africa Line became known as Farrell Lines, whose main rivals on the long haul from North America to Southern Africa were Lykes Lines and the Robin Line. Today Lykes Lines and United States Lines, who took over Moore McCormack recently, are still engaged on this route ■

1 The *African Comet* arriving in Table Bay harbour on 20 Sep-tember 1962 after a record-breaking run from New York at an average speed of 22,31 knots. This vessel was the first of six fast steamers which Farrell Lines had built for the service to

2

Southern Africa. During the Vietnam War several vessels of this class were used as transports.

2 The *African Crescent* was typical of Farrell Lines' immediate post-war ships. They were of a class known as C-2 and were eventually replaced by the *African Comet*-class in the early 1960s.

3 The *Velma Lykes* was a turbine steamer of a class built during the Second World War and seen regularly in South African waters during the 1950s and early 1960s.

4 Built in 1963, the *Aimee Lykes* ran aground on the Aliwal Shoal near Durban on her maiden voyage. This presented the local ship-repair industry with one of its biggest contracts. In recent years some of the vessels of this class – with their rather unusual split superstructure and twin funnels – have been lengthened to transport containers.

5 The *Robin Goodfellow,* a Robin Line steamer with a C-2 hull, was built in 1945 and called regularly at South African ports.

4

THE SOUTH AFRICAN government has owned and operated ocean-going cargo ships since the end of the First World War, when three war-prize vessels of 5 000 tons were registered under the South African flag. They were the twin-funnelled *Apolda*, the *Huntress* and the *Seattle*. The main function of these ships was to transport railway sleepers from Australia. In later years a triangular service developed, with the export of coal to ports in the Far East. Occasional voyages to Europe were made, mainly with cargoes of maize. Between 1925 and 1931 the original ships were replaced by three new vessels of 8 900 d.w.t. After the Second World War the number of SAR cargo ships diminished, the last vessel, the *Johan Hugo*, being sold in 1984 ∎

1 Originally a German vessel, the *Huntress* was handed over to the government of South Africa in 1919 as a war prize. While carrying coal to the Far East she was badly damaged in a collision in the Straits of Singapore.

2 The first of the new ships built for the South African government, the *Aloe* was completed in 1925. She was torpedoed in April 1943 by the German submarine *U-182* in a position about 800 kilometres east of Durban.

3 The German-built *Apolda* became a war prize in Table Bay in 1914.

4 The *Erica,* built in 1926, replaced the obsolete *Apolda* on the Australian run. Throughout her career she encountered problems – a fire in her bunkers, aground on Vankoro Island, severely damaged by bad weather near Australia. In 1951, as the *Neptune Star,* she became structurally unsound and was scrapped.

5 With the departure of the *Erica* and the *Agulhas* in the early 1950s, the only SAR vessels that remained were the *Dalia* and the second *Aloe*. But age was creating increasing problems and the *Aloe* was also sold. After this there were several chartered ships, unfortunately of similar vintage and condition. In 1956 another war-built steamer, the *Hangklip,* came under the SAR's green and gold livery. When the *Dalia* departed in 1959, only the *Hangklip* remained.

6 In 1966 the SAR acquired a new 12 000 d.w.t. Japanese-built bulk carrier, the *Johan Hugo*. A rather small vessel compared with modern bulk carriers, she transported coal along the South African seaboard for eighteen years and was the last cargo ship to be operated by the SAR.

AFTER the second World War a number of South African shipping companies were established, but for various reasons most of them soon disappeared. However, as a result of astute management and timely mergers, two companies have survived: the South African Marine Corporation (Safmarine) and Unicorn Lines.

In 1947 Safmarine inaugurated a cargo service to the United States with three war-built 'Victory' steamers. In the mid-1950s four new steamers were added to the fleet. In 1959 the Industrial Development Corporation took over the shares in Safmarine that had belonged to the States Marine Corporation of America, and in 1961 a merger with Springbok Shipping Company increased the fleet to fourteen ships.

Safmarine's first bulk carrier was acquired in 1965 and was the forerunner of the fleet of bulk carriers owned by the Corporation today. During the 1960s, six refrigerated ships and eight dry-cargo liners came into service. The latter, which replaced older vessels, put Safmarine firmly on the world shipping map as their speed enabled them to compete successfully with rival freighters. Political problems curtailed the Corporation's entry into the tanker field.

With the phasing in of containerization since 1977, many of Safmarine's conventional break-bulk cargo liners have been sold and replaced by six large cellular vessels, which serve Britain, north-western Europe, the Mediterranean and the Far East. There is also a semi-containerized service to ports in North America ■

1 The launching of the steamer *South African Merchant* in Scotland in December 1954 was an important milestone in the growth of Safmarine. The 9 500-

ton vessel was the first of four similar ships, the remaining three being acquired in 1956.

2 The *South African Victory* was one of the original trio of war-built 'Victory' ships that entered the monthly service from the United States to South Africa in 1947. They were originally named the *Vergelegen*, the *Morgenster* and the *Constantia* and were the pioneers of the Safmarine fleet.

3 In 1962 Safmarine decided to enter the lucrative field of refrigerated shipping. Their first reefer, the *Langkloof*, was built in Holland in 1963, and during the same year three similar ships were constructed on the Clyde. The first of these was the *Letaba*, followed by the *Drakenstein* and the *Tzaneen*. These vessels were taken on bare-boat charter by Safmarine. Three years later the

S.A. Hexrivier was launched on the Maas in Holland (see photograph). The final ship in the series, the *S.A. Zebediela,* came into service in 1968.

4 The *South African Merchant* served the company well and was scrapped only in 1977, after twenty-two years in Safmarine colours.

1 When the three American lines introduced their faster ships, built with government aid in the early 1960s, Safmarine envisaged severe competition. As the world-wide shipping recession was coming to an end, the company embarked on a major replacement and expansion programme. The first of eight new liners to enter service was the Dutch-built *S.A. van der Stel*, which arrived in Cape Town in August 1966. This vessel presented a new look, having a long foredeck dominated by two massive heavy-lift derricks.

2 Five of the eight new cargo liners were built in Japan and the original names *Constantia*, *Morgenster* and *Vergelegen* were revived. The *S.A. Constantia* is pictured here in Hamburg. In December 1969 the *S.A. Vergelegen,* the last of the new ships, docked in Cape Town, just over three years after the arrival of the *S.A. van der Stel.*

3 A containerized shipping service between Europe and South Africa was investigated by the government-appointed Steenkamp Commission in the late 1960s. The official announcement for the go-ahead

2 500 TEUs each. The photograph shows the first vessel of this class, the *S.A. Helderberg*, which arrived in March 1978.

5 The second ship of the Helderberg-class to be completed was the 49 000 d.w.t. *S.A. Sederberg*. Both vessels have two eight-cylinder Sulzer diesels developing nearly 20 000 kW each, and can carry some 900 refrigerated containers.

6 During the mid-1970s it became necessary to lengthen the break-bulk ships built between 1966 and 1969. A cellular section forward of the superstructure was inserted, enabling each ship to carry 200 TEUs. The photograph shows the *S.A. Alphen* in the Far East.

was made jointly by the Secretary for Commerce and the chairman of the Europe/South and South East Africa Conference in March 1974. At this stage Safmarine's plans for container ships were well advanced, and in July 1974 the Corporation announced that a medium-sized cellular vessel had been ordered from Italy. The 23 500 d.w.t. *S.A. Langeberg* (shown here), which arrived in Cape Town in July 1977 and inaugurated a new era in shipping in South Africa, has a container capacity of nearly 1 400 TEUs and a maximum speed of 21 knots.

4 The major order for container vessels went to French shipyards. This contract, worth about R300 million, was for four ships capable of carrying about

1 To facilitate a quick turn-round in port, the handling of containers continues throughout the night. Departures and arrivals of container vessels take place at any hour of the day or night, weather permitting.

2 The lucrative route from South Africa to the Far East was the next to be containerized. Safmarine is a partner in the Safari Service, which operates with four cellular ships – two Japanese, one Dutch and the 34 000 d.w.t. *S.A. Vaal*. Built at a cost of R40 million, the *S.A. Vaal* entered service in July 1982 and is shown here during her sea trials.

3 The first bulk carrier to fly Safmarine colours was the 24 000 d.w.t. *Sugela*, initially employed to transport sugar to Japan. Six similar vessels were built in Japanese shipyards between 1973 and 1979, the

Victory, shown here at New York, being the last. A much larger bulk carrier, the 165 000 d.w.t. *Sishen,* owned jointly by Safmarine and Iscor, is employed on the iron-ore trade from Saldanha Bay to Japan. A construction programme involving new bulk carriers is being completed.

4 The bridge of a modern container ship has a functional, uncluttered appearance.

5 Similar conditions prevail in the engine control room, which is air-conditioned and virtually soundproof. The officer on watch has banks of switches, dials and lights to monitor, and the aim is eventually to have an engine room that is unmanned for sixteen hours.

6 There is a complete contrast between the modern vessels on this page and this 'Liberty' ship, plodding along the coast. Hundreds of these utility vessels were built during the Second World War in North America, the shipyards there breaking all construction records. Although these all-welded, rather sluggish cargo vessels were intended for war service only, many survived well into the 1960s.

7 The *Rockhampton Star,* a Blue Star Line vessel built in 1958. Ships belonging to this company were used in former years mainly for shipping frozen meat from Argentina, Australia and New Zealand to Britain. Since the war, Blue Star vessels have regularly called at South African ports to load export fruit.

8 Further rationalization of the Union-Castle mail service in 1965, which included the withdrawal of three pre-war passenger mailships, resulted in the construction of two cargo ships, the *Southampton Castle* (shown here) and the *Good Hope Castle.* Both vessels had large refrigerated spaces, and after they were obliged to call at the islands of St Helena and Ascension accommodation for 12 passengers was added. Two powerful Sulzer diesel engines and a streamlined hull enabled these ships to attain a service speed of over 22 knots, which was necessary for the new 11½ day mail schedule. At the time they were the most powerful cargo motor-ships afloat.

1 The *Eiken Maru,* built in 1952, was owned by the Nippon Yusen Kaisha (NYK), the first Japanese shipping company to provide a regular service to South Africa. In 1904 one of its ships put into Durban, en route to Rio de Janeiro, and in 1916 it started a regular six-weekly schedule with the *Wakasa Maru.* A large number of emigrants from Japan to Brazil were aboard most of its vessels that called between the wars.

Another Japanese line, the Osaka Shosen Kaisha (OSK), began to compete with the NYK in 1917 by introducing a round-the-world service. Some fine ships belonging to the OSK, such as the *Santos Maru* and the *Rio de Janeiro Maru,* both with excellent passenger accommodation, were seen in South African ports. In 1931, during the great economic depression, the rationalization of Japanese shipping led to the withdrawal of the NYK from the South African route and its replacement by the OSK.

After the Second World War, Japanese companies resumed regular cargo services to Southern Africa with fast modern vessels. At present the large container ship *Osaka Maru* is on the South African run.
2 The *Nedlloyd Kembla* and her sister ships are engaged on a Nedlloyd Line round-the-world service, calling at South African, U.S. Gulf, Central American and Australian ports. The *Nedlloyd Kembla* was built in Japan in 1971.
3 Lloyd Triestino of Trieste operate a regular container service from Mediterranean ports to South Africa in conjunction with Safmarine. The Italian ships *Africa* (seen here) and *Europa* are sister ships to the *S.A. Langeberg.* .The *Africa* was the first custom-built

container ship to enter the Southern Africa/Europe Container Service (SAECS) in 1977. They are turbine steamers with a speed of 21 knots and can carry nearly 1 400 TEUs. Lloyd Triestino, though better known for their passenger liners, have connected the Mediterranean and Southern Africa with their cargo vessels since the beginning of this century.

4 Bearing the same name as an earlier Ellerman and Bucknall passenger/cargo liner (see photograph on page 90), the present *City of Durban* is a 47 000 d.w.t. container vessel which entered service in 1978. She was built in Bremen and is owned jointly by Ellerman Lines Ltd and the Charente Steamship Company (Harrison's). A sister ship to the *Table Bay,* built for

Overseas Container Lines, she is powered by MAN diesels.

5 Thor Dahl of Sandefjord in Norway, who has operated the Christensen Canadian African Line since 1948, was actively involved in whaling for many years, hence the stylized blue whale on the houseflag and funnel of his vessels. The *Thorshope,* built in 1958, was typical of the cargo liners used by the company in the 1950s and 1960s. The Thor ships, which were usually in immaculate condition, had accommodation for twelve passengers. At present the line's monthly service is operated by two fast, multi-purpose cargo vessels of 20 000 d.w.t.

6 The container ship *Transvaal,* owned by Deutsche-Afrika Linie, is generally similar to the other large ships of this type described on previous pages. She is fitted with equipment for satellite navigation and has the distinction of being the largest motor-ship in the German merchant fleet.

1,2 One of fourteen new shipping companies that were formed during and immediately after the Second World War was the Cape Town-based South African Lines. Originally the company operated chartered vessels to South America and West Africa, but in 1947 an 8 000 d.w.t. motor-ship was acquired and renamed *Kaapland*. Two years later another two vessels were registered in Cape Town and given the names *Namaqualand* and *Damaraland*. Subsequently a regular service to north-western Europe was introduced. Some years after Deutsche Ost-Afrika Linie had resumed trading to South Africa, three of their ships were renamed *Mossel Bay*, *Table Bay* and *Walvis Bay* and a joint service with South African Lines came into operation.

The bottom photograph shows the first *Kaapland*, formerly the *Vasaland*. The top photograph shows the second *Kaapland*, which was completed in 1959. She was a motor-ship of 10 300 d.w.t. with a service speed of 18 knots.

In 1973 South African Lines was taken over by Safmarine.

3 The South African coasting service had its origin in 1838 when the 194-ton paddle steamer *Hope* arrived from Scottish builders for the Cape of Good Hope Steam Navigation Company, which traded between Cape Town and Algoa Bay. Unfortunately the venture came

3

4

5

6

to an early end when the vessel was wrecked at Cape St Francis after only fifteen months. Other small vessels followed, including the *Sir Robert Peel,* which in 1852 became the first steamer to cross the bar at Durban.

During the 1850s and 1860s the Barrys of Swellendam developed Port Beaufort at the mouth of the Breede River, and their small coasters made regular voyages from Cape Town to Malgas, 30 km upstream from Port Beaufort. However, the port was closed in 1865 and it was not until 1935 that an attempt was made to resume the Breede River service. The 170-ton former water-tanker *Chub* (shown in the photograph) was used for this purpose. Built in 1899, she transported bagged wheat from the Swellendam area and took petroleum products in drums, as well as general cargo, from Cape

Town. She was later switched to the Port Nolloth run, but was lost after running aground at Cape St Martin.

4 The first *Nahoon,* owned by Smith's Coasters, was built in Scotland in 1935.

5 The *Voortrekker* arrived from her Scottish builders in 1947.

She was owned by African Coasters and spent almost her entire twenty-two year career coasting between Durban, East London and Port Elizabeth.

6 The 540-ton steamer *Karatara* was acquired by Thesens in 1913 and was in service for eight years.

1

2

3

4

EARLY IN THE 1960s THERE were four coasting companies operating along the South African seaboard: Thesens Steamship Company, Smith's Coasters, African Coasters and Durban Lines. By the mid-1960s a surge in the economy and the total relaxation of railway competition resulted in much additional cargo becoming available. As most of the vessels in use had not been built specifically for the coastal trade, replacements were needed. In 1964 African Coasters exchanged shareholdings with a leading mining company, Union Corporation Ltd, and six modern ships were acquired. Smith's replaced their fleet with eight modern vessels. In 1965 Safmarine bought a controlling shareholding in Thesens. During the following year African Coasters and Smith's merged to form Unicorn Shipping Holdings, African Coasters becoming the principal operating company and changing its name to Unicorn Lines. Safmarine later sold Thesens to Unicorn and eventually acquired a large percentage of Unicorn's share capital. Since the late 1960s Unicorn has built up a fleet of modern ships suited to the requirements of its various trades. Some foreign services have been pioneered by Unicorn, notably those to South America, Israel and various islands in the Indian Ocean ■

1 When official railway competition was removed in 1954, a number of old ships were bought at low prices for the growing coastal trade. The *Range* was one of these and provided a slow service mainly between Cape Town and Durban. When capital became available to the coasting trade in the mid-1960s new ships were acquired to replace these obsolete vessels.
2 The sister ship to the first *Nahoon* was the first *Gamtoos,*

which arrived in South Africa from the builders in 1937. She was requisitioned by the Admiralty in 1942 and served as a salvage vessel in the Mediterranean, only returning to commercial duties in 1947. During part of this period she was commanded by Lieutenant H. Biermann, who later became head of the South African Defence Force. For the rest of her working life, which ended in 1973, she was employed as a guano vessel between Cape Town and the West Coast guano islands. A three-year lay-up period ended when she was scuttled off the Cape Peninsula.
3 The 15 650 d.w.t. *Umfolozi,* Unicorn Lines' biggest general cargo ship, was built in Japan in

1978. This multi-purpose vessel was bought for R8,5 million, and entered Unicorn's Israel service in 1980. A Burmeister and Wain diesel gives her a speed of 16 knots.
4 Unicorn Lines' largest vessel, the 33 000 d.w.t. Italian-built tanker *Buffalo,* was bought in 1977 as a replacement for the company's previous coastal tanker, the *Africa Shell.*
5 In the mid-1970s there was a need for more ships to transport the increasing number of containers on the coastal service. Two extended Trampco-type multi-purpose vessels of about 8 000 tons were ordered from Durban shipyards. The second *Gamtoos* was the first of these to enter service, in 1976.

5

1 In 1975 the Texaco tanker fleet consisted of about eighty ships registered in Britain, the United States, Norway and Panama. The 210 000 d.w.t. *Texaco North America* was photographed outside port limits off Cape Town in 1970. She was one of the hundreds of tankers to be serviced by Table Bay ferry boats.
2 As the coasting trade became more lucrative in the late 1950s and early 1960s, all the remaining coal-fired coasters were replaced by motor-ships.

The engine room of Unicorn Lines' *Ridge* is seen here.
3 The 16 800 d.w.t *Caltex Glasgow* was a unit of the colossal United States ship-building programme during the Second World War. Of the basic T2-SE-A1 design, 481 tankers were built at four different shipyards. A further 44 were of a slightly different design and, having more power, they achieved 16 knots with their turbo-electric machinery. The *Caltex Glasgow* was built by the Kaiser Company in 1945.

4 When the world's demand for oil increased dramatically in the early 1950s, the size of tankers grew correspondingly. The handsome *Tina Onassis,* ordered by Aristotle Onassis from Hamburg Shipbuilders, was, at 45 750 d.w.t., the largest tanker in the world when completed in 1953. Her carrying capacity was nearly three times that of a T-2 tanker. She would of course be dwarfed by today's 300 000 tonners.
5 With freight rates at an all-time high, Safmarine ordered three VLCCs (very large crude carriers) from Japanese shipyards. The 220 000 d.w.t. *Kulu* was completed in 1971 and carried oil from the Persian Gulf to Europe on charter to an oil company. She and her sister ship, the *Gondwana,* were sold in 1979. The third vessel, the *Sinde,* was sold soon after completion in 1973.
6 In April 1981 the 205 000 d.w.t. Liberian tanker *Energy Endurance,* owned by C.Y. Tung, was bound for Europe with a full cargo of crude oil when she was apparently hit by an abnormal wave off East London. On inspection it was established that the forepeak tank had collapsed, leaving a gaping hole about 13 metres square on both the port and starboard sides.

ALTHOUGH containerization was introduced in the 1970s, conventional methods of cargo handling have not been neglected but have been mechanized and automated. The recently developed bulk-export harbours of Saldanha Bay and Richard's Bay have had the most modern equipment installed for bulk loading in order to achieve a speedy turn-round for the large bulk-carriers frequenting these ports. To facilitate the discharge of bulk cargoes, mechanized crane grabs have been introduced for handling maize, fertilizer and other bulk imports.

Two additional developments in the field of conventional cargo handling in recent years have been the palletization of export fruit and the introduction of ro-ro-type vessels for the movement of motor vehicles. For shipowners it has become imperative to keep a vessel's length of stay in port to a minimum, so as to reduce port dues and increase the number of round voyages. Modern methods of cargo handling, such as containerization, ro-ro, LASH and others, have helped ship-owners to offset high operating costs and reduce losses.

Since the introduction of containerization there has been a steady increase in the number of TEUs handled by coastal shipping. In 1983 nearly 60% of all coastal cargo was in containers ■

1 Rolls of newsprint produced by the Sappi mills are shipped to coastal ports from Durban by such vessels as Unicorn Lines' *Kowie,* a Trampco-type ship that has been on the coast since 1983.
2 A large proportion of South Africa's perishable exports, e.g. deciduous and citrus fruit, is now containerized and shipped by fully cellular ships. The balance of export cargoes is palletized and handled by the conventional method.
3 The amount of break-bulk cargo in relation to containerized cargo is slowly diminishing. However, West Coast ports such as Port Nolloth and Lüderitz handle only break-bulk cargoes at present. Examples of cargo shipped from South African ports in this way are consignments of timber, bales of wool, liquids in drums and cartons of fruit.
4 Most containers are of a standard size known as a TEU (Twenty Foot Equivalent Unit). The container terminals are usually far removed from the

rest of the harbour, which precludes the general public from observing the handling methods of this revolutionary system.

5 Containers enter the harbour by special lorry and are taken to a 'stacking' area to await the arrival of the ship. When loading is in progress a fleet of lorries brings the containers alongside the ship, underneath the giant gantry cranes. These cranes have automatic coupling devices enabling the crane operator to secure, lift and disconnect the container. On board the container ships there are automatic devices that lock the containers in the lower layers in place. Those carried on deck are secured with additional lashing to avoid movement when at sea.

Although the initial investment to finance the switch to containerization has been heavy, it should, in the long term, be compensated for by the many advantages of the system. Some of these advantages are: cargo handling time has been reduced to less than a quarter of the time needed for the break-bulk method; containers are handled in all weather conditions; and pilfering of freight has virtually been eradicated.

6 Drums lashed together in the pre-container era on the fore-deck of the passenger/cargo liner *Jagersfontein* of the Holland-Afrika Lijn, which is now integrated into Nedlloyd Lines' services.

7 The Moore McCormack multi-purpose cargo liner *Mormacaltair,* shown at the Durban container terminal. The company has recently been absorbed by United States Lines, which has renamed the Moore McCormack liners, in each case using the prefix *American.*

127

1 With the introduction of the so-called third generation ro-ro (roll on-roll off) ships at the end of the 1970s, a new dimension was added to South African shipping services. The ro-ro concept is a development of the ferry services that exist in various parts of the world and is an extension of road transportation. The photograph shows the massive angled quarter-ramp of the *Kolsnaren*. This ramp, which weighs about 400 tons and is nearly 50 metres long, takes about 30 minutes to lower and is wide enough for two-way traffic. Fork-lift trucks and trucks with trailers are able to handle all the cargo that needs

shipping, a series of ramps making it possible for the lowest deck to be reached by vehicles driven aboard from the quayside. Containers are also stacked on the weather deck.
2 The view from a gantry crane, showing a container being placed in its allotted position aboard a container vessel. The complete operation is computerized and the location of each container can be ascertained at any time.
3 An everyday sight at the container terminals in Cape Town, Durban and Port Elizabeth: a fully cellular vessel, and the smooth and efficient operation of loading or

discharging it. One gantry crane handles on average twenty-five containers an hour, which means about 600 tons of cargo.

4 The Sishen-Saldanha project, which received the South African Institute of Civil Engineers' award for the most outstanding civil engineering project of 1976, is earning valuable foreign exchange for South Africa. At present, ore carriers of up to 250 000 d.w.t. load at Saldanha Bay. The ore is transported from Sishen, 861 kilometres away, by ore trains that have a length exceeding 2 kilometres. The mine at Sishen produces about 25 million tons of ore annually.

5 The first ro-ro car carriers on the South African coastal service were the *Greta Delport* and the *Zwartkops*, both of which entered service in 1969. The latter ferried about 300 vehicles per voyage between the major coastal ports for ten years. A much larger vessel, the *Mkuze* (shown here), was purchased by Unicorn Lines in 1979 and is still in use. Nearly 58 000 new vehicles were transported by sea in 1982 from the ports of assembly to the other major ports in South Africa.

NOT SINCE THE SECOND World War had South African ports been called upon to service and supply such a large and varied number of ships, as during the first closure of the Suez Canal in 1956-7. The nationalization of the canal by Egypt in 1956 led to an invasion of that country by an Anglo-French force. In the resulting conflict a large number of ships were sunk and blocked the canal.

South African ports bore the brunt of the diverted traffic and congestion was inevitable. At times dozens of vessels were swinging at anchor, mainly off Cape Town and Durban. Many large liners from the Indian, Far East and Australian routes called for bunkers and stores, allowing their passengers an unscheduled visit to South Africa. The diversion around the Cape added weeks to the voyages of cargo liners, tramps and tankers, and shipping companies had to charter additional tonnage to keep to their schedules. However, in 1957 the canal was cleared fairly rapidly and conditions returned to normal.

A decade later the canal was blocked once more when ships were sunk during the Arab-Israeli war of 1967. This time it remained closed for eight years. Within weeks of the closure an unprecedented armada of ships converged on South African ports. Harbour staffs worked round the clock and vessels were double- and triple-berthed. Not unexpectedly, the number of collisions, strandings and general breakdowns increased, resulting in a boom period for ship repairers and chandlers. The off-shore launch and helicopter services came into their own, and scores of ships, each with a large bunker capacity, called off-limits, mainly in Table Bay, to take on essential supplies, as well as spares, films and mail. Later, crew members were exchanged

in South Africa and an increasing number of shipowners utilized this facility. The jaded tanker crews on the Persian Gulf run were particularly appreciative of 'the shop at the corner', which became the highlight of their monotonous five week-trip around Africa.

Another phenomenon of this period was the rapid growth in

the size of oil tankers. Because of the longer haul around Africa, more tonnage was needed to supply crude oil to the industrial nations of the West. Shipyards enlarged their slipways and dock capacities to build VLCC's (very large crude carriers) and ULCC's (ultra large crude carriers), the majority ranging in deadweight capacity from 150 000 to 300 000

CHAPTER
VI
SUEZ CLOSURES

tons, though a few in excess of this tonnage were built. But then the oil crisis hit the world, and, with the re-opening of the canal in 1975, freight rates tumbled. This resulted in scores of tankers moving to lay-up berths, and in many being scrapped barely ten years after completion.

The closure of the canal, with its resultant increase in traffic

around the Cape, brought salvage contractors to the area, who stationed large tugs at Cape Town, Durban and Mombasa. South Africa later obtained its own large salvage vessels in the form of the Safmarine giants, *S.A. John Ross* and *S.A. Wolraad Woltemade*.

After two world wars and two Suez crises the strategic

importance of the Cape route and the excellent port facilities in South Africa have become recognized by the maritime nations of the Western world ■

1 It was very common during both Suez closures to see ships berthed at every available quay, especially in Durban and Cape Town.

1 The Orient Line built five 20 000-ton passenger liners for the Australian trade between 1924 and 1929. The *Orontes* (shown here) was the last of the quintet to be completed by Vickers-Armstrongs. With her sister ship, the *Otranto,* she survived the war, doing troopship duties for seven years. After a refit she carried 1 100 passengers in two classes until 1953, when she was converted into a tourist-class liner. She called at Cape Town during the first Suez closure and again in 1961, when she carried immigrants to Australia via the Cape to avoid the heat of the Middle East (she lacked air-conditioning). The following year this graceful ship was scrapped.

1

2 Heading out with supplies to a ship passing off-limits is a wooden-hulled, sturdily built supply vessel. Although a helicopter service has been in operation for some years, these small craft are still a part of the scene at Table Bay. They are crewed by seasoned men who will go out in most weather conditions, transporting anything from spare parts to Christmas trees.

3 Built by Harland and Wolff for the Royal Mail Line's service between England and La Plata, the *Asturias* was of the same period and size as the *Orontes* and was powered by diesel engines. She originally had accommodation for 1 400 passengers in three classes. To achieve a higher speed she was lengthened, her funnels were increased in height, and steam turbines replaced the diesels. Her forward funnel was removed in 1939 and she was converted into an armed merchant cruiser. While serving in the South Atlantic in 1943 she was torpedoed by the Italian submarine *Cagni,* and badly damaged. After a lay-up period in Freetown she was sold to the Admiralty and converted into a troopship in 1947. As such she called at Cape Town during the first Suez closure.

4 The *Empire Fowey,* built in 1935 as the fast turbo-electric passenger/cargo liner *Potsdam* for the Far East trade of its owners, Hamburg-Amerika Linie. However, she was sold in the same year to Norddeutscher Lloyd to join two similar liners on the Far East route. During the war she was used as an accommodation ship in Hamburg and Gotenhafen, and in 1945 she took part in the evacuation of the German eastern provinces. Allocated to Britain after the war, she served as the troopship *Empire Jewel* and later the *Empire Fowey.* Under this name she called at Cape Town in 1957, during the first Suez crisis. In 1960 she hoisted the Pakistani flag and was renamed *Safina-E-Hujjaj,* to carry pilgrims to Jiddah and passengers to Hong Kong and East Africa.

2

1 The *Orsova*, the third and last passenger liner of Orient Line's immediate post-war replacement programme. Completed in 1954 by Vickers-Armstrongs, this 29 000-ton ship was the largest at the time with an all-welded hull and appeared somewhat bare without conventional masts. Built for the England-Australasia route, she originally carried 1 500 passengers and about half that number during cruises in the latter part of a

relatively short career, which ended in 1974.

2 The *Achille Lauro,* a striking passenger liner which was ordered by Rotterdam Lloyd before the last war but only completed by De Schelde shipyard in 1947. Known then as the *Willem Ruys,* she was placed on the service to the East Indies. After the independence of Indonesia she was switched to a round-the-world route in 1959 following an extensive refit. In

1965 the Italian Flotta Lauro acquired the liner and drastically changed her appearance. Until 1972 she was on the company's service to Australia and New Zealand, carrying about 1 300 passengers. Her final ten years were spent cruising to various parts of the world.

3 With the exception of Union-Castle Line's heyday, it was a rare occurrence to have three passenger liners of the same

company berthed in Table Bay harbour. This event happened in 1972 when the two Lloyd Triestino express liners, *Galileo Galilei* and *Guglielmo Marconi* on the Italy-Australia route, and the smaller *Europa,* were in port simultaneously. The two express liners carried about 1 700 passengers at 24 knots. They were built in 1963 and withdrawn after only fourteen years in service. Some attempts at cruising were made, but both have been laid up since 1981.

4 Photographed in Table Bay harbour in 1972, the *Uruguay Star* was on her way to the Far East to be scrapped. On closer inspection she revealed comfortable accommodation for about 50 passengers. Built for the Blue Star Line with three sister ships in 1947/8, this 10 700 ton liner had large refrigerated spaces for use on the meat trade from South America. These ships served their entire careers on the London-Buenos Aires route.

1 The former North Atlantic liner *America* (shown here as the *Australis*) has had a long and varied career. Commissioned by United States Lines in 1940, she first cruised to the West Indies but became a troopship the following year. When transferred to the United States Navy she was renamed *West Point*. After the war she underwent an extensive refit and entered the North Atlantic service carrying about 1 000 passengers. Purchased by Chandris Lines of Piraeus in 1964, she reappeared

the following year in the distinctive livery of her new owners and with the name *Australis*. The one-class accommodation had been increased to over 2 000 berths. She was sold by Chandris in 1978 and her new owners revived the old name *America*. Chandris then repurchased her for cruising in the Mediterranean and gave her the name *Italis*. Finally, in 1980, she was sold to a Swiss concern for use as a floating hotel.

2 Scores of tankers of the VLCC type called off-limits in Table Bay during the second Suez closure. The 209 000 d.w.t. Greek-owned *Evgenia Chandris* was built in 1969, and is shown here in ballast that year being approached by the Cape Town-based supply vessel.

3 The P. and O. liner *Canberra*, built in 1961, made her South African debut in June 1967, calling at Cape Town for bunkers. When she entered service she reduced the passage from England to Australia by one week. She has been used entirely for cruising since 1973, with the exception of a period in 1982 when she acted as a hospital ship and troopship during the Falklands War.

4 Ships of the Soviet-bloc countries are not frequent visitors to South African ports. However, during the Suez crises many types of cargo vessels called for bunkers and stores. The Polish-owned *Hanka Sawicka* (shown here) is one of a class of eleven similar vessels built in Gdansk during the early 1960s.

SHIPWRECKS along the coast of Southern Africa were first recorded in the 1550s, a century before Jan van Riebeeck arrived in Table Bay. According to reliable sources the first of these recorded disasters was the *San Jerome,* which went aground north of the mouth of the Mhlatuze River near the present Richard's Bay. Since then more than 1 200 ships have been wrecked on or near the coast, and countless vessels have been involved in less serious accidents. Until the construction of sheltered harbours a large proportion of the losses were due to inadequate protection of anchored vessels against storms.

The other main causes of maritime disaster along our coastline have been inaccurate charts, a lack of lighthouses in earlier years, poorly constructed ships, severe weather conditions, wartime hostilities, mechanical failure and, of course, human fallibility ■

CHAPTER VII

MARITIME CASUALTIES

1 On the night of 31 May 1773 there was tempestuous weather in Table Bay. A north-wester had been raging for days and several Dutch East India Company ships were at anchor, riding out the storm. The *De Jonge Thomas,* with over 200 men aboard, lost all her anchors and was driven ashore near the Salt River mouth during the early hours of the following day. The ship started to break up almost immediately, though many of her crew managed to cling to the wreckage. At dawn Wolraad Woltemade, an inhabitant of Cape Town who had ridden down to the scene, urged his horse into the sea a number of times to rescue the survivors. He succeeded in saving fourteen of them before he and his exhausted animal were pulled under by panicking sailors.

Wolraad Woltemade's heroic action has since passed into legend and one of the giant Safmarine salvage tugs is named after him.

1,2 On 14 August 1902, besides the *City of Lincoln* and the *Highfields*, the sailing vessel *Brutus* was driven ashore in Table Bay at almost the same spot where she had grounded thirteen years previously as the *Sierra Pedrosa*. She was re-floated and spent the rest of her life as a coal hulk in Table Bay.

3 The Aberdeen White Star liner *Thermopylae*, named after the famous clipper, was built in 1891 for the service to Australia via the Cape. In September 1899, homeward bound with fifty passengers aboard, she ran aground close to the Green Point lighthouse in Table Bay. It was a calm night and the passengers

and crew were brought safely ashore. Carcasses of frozen meat from her holds were washed onto the beaches, but most of her cargo of gold coins was salvaged.

4 The *Clan Monroe* was one of a class of seven turret ships built for Clan Line in 1897/8. On a voyage from Liverpool to Delagoa Bay in July 1905, she

ventured too close to Slangkop
Point and was wrecked.

5 The *Orient,* a Russian sailing
ship with auxiliary engines,
aground on the East London
waterfront early this century.
Other ships, notably the *Galway
Castle,* the *Valdivia* and the *S.A.
Oranjeland,* also came to grief
not far from here.

6 The Shaw Savill and Albion
Company steamer *Maori,* built in
1893, left Table Bay shortly
before midnight on 4 August
1909 and headed into a typical
midwinter north-west gale. The
wind, combined with the current,
forced her off course and she was
driven onto the rocks close to
Duiker Point, an uninhabited

stretch of coastline near Hout
Bay. Three boats were launched,
but only one reached safety.
Subsequently a tug was
dispatched from Cape Town, but
the heavy seas prevented her
from going in close. It was not
until two days later that the
remaining survivors could be
rescued.

desert coastline, which has moved seaward with the advance of the sand dunes.

3 Another Woermann liner, the second *Gertrud Woermann*, became a total loss near Swakopmund when she went aground in fog. At the time she was a troop transport during the Herero uprising. She was built in England for Norddeutscher Lloyd as the *Pfalz* in 1893.

4 Algoa Bay's great shipping disaster occurred on 1 September 1902. Thirty-eight vessels were anchored in the bay when a south-west gale reached hurricane force, driving twenty ashore, with great loss of life.

5 The 9 300-ton liner *Waratah*, built for the Blue Anchor Line's Australian service via the Cape, was bound for London in July 1909 when she called at Durban for coal bunkers and cargo, and to embark passengers. She left Durban on 26 July for Cape Town and exchanged signals early the next day with the *Clan Macintyre*. That was the last time she was seen. Other ships reported heavy weather in the area, and the most likely explanation for her disappearance is that she was hit by a giant wave and capsized. No wreckage was ever found, or the bodies of any of the 211 people on board.

1 Originally built as the transatlantic liner *Manhattan* for the Guion Line of New York in 1886, the *City of Lincoln* became a total wreck on Woodstock Beach, Table Bay, in 1902.

2 Before running aground in thick fog near Walvis Bay in 1909, the Woermann Linie steamer *Eduard Bohlen* had maintained the coastal service between the Cape and South West Africa for six years. The photograph, taken in 1960, shows her remains several hundred metres inshore of the

1 The small coaster *Umzimvubu*, the second vessel owned by C.G. Smith, traded between Durban and Port St Johns from 1886. The photograph shows her aground near the Umgeni River mouth after running out of fuel. She was refloated and continued in Smith's service until he sold her to Thesens, who renamed her *Namaqua*.

2 The Dutch coaster *Frean*, built in Holland in 1940 as the *Erna*, was taken on charter by Thesens in 1954 to assist with the movement of increased volumes of cargo. Her coastal trips came to an abrupt end when she was lost on the desert coast at Port Nolloth in August 1957.

3 Two tugs attempting to refloat the British freighter *Dunbath*, aground at Lüderitz in 1907.

The inhospitable desert coast of South West Africa, known as the Skeleton Coast north of Walvis Bay, has claimed many ships over the years. In November 1942 the Blue Star liner *Dunedin Star*, laden with war supplies, struck bottom and was beached more than 600 kilometres north of Walvis Bay.

Rescue was difficult owing to the remoteness of the area. A plane actually landed on the beach but was bogged down. Eventually the passengers and crew were rescued by military vehicles. The 40-year-old Walvis Bay tug *Sir Charles Elliott* was sent north to render assistance, but on her return trip she was herself wrecked near Rocky Point about 500 kilometres north of Walvis Bay.

4 The Thesens coaster *Basuto Coast* was approaching Cape Town early on 19 May 1954 when her fuel pump failed during a severe storm. Both anchors were dropped but the cables parted and the little ship was left to the mercy of wind and wave. Before a tug could reach

her she was driven ashore, so close to the Sea Point swimming pool that the crew were saved by the fire brigade using ladders.

5 The small coaster *Nolloth,* built in 1936 in Holland as the *Alpha,* was chartered by African Coasters in 1963. After rounding the Cape she apparently struck a submerged object and, making water, was put ashore near Olifants Point, her crew being rescued by helicopter. The site of her grounding was close to the remains of the *Thomas T. Tucker,* a Liberty ship wrecked during the Second World War.

1 The Ellerman liner *City of Lincoln* made headlines in 1946 when she ran aground at Quoin Point while travelling at full speed. Having come through the notorious Malta convoys in the Second World War, she was an important vessel in the Ellerman fleet and everything possible was done to refloat her. Salvage experts sealed off all open spaces and pumped air into the ship, thus refloating her on a cushion of air. The tug *T.S. McEwen* towed her to Cape Town, where she was brought into the Duncan Dock stern first. On inspection in dry dock she was found to be so badly damaged that it was decided not to repair her.

2 On 1 April 1947 the Greek cargo ship *George M. Livanos* ran aground during the small hours of the morning in good weather conditions virtually within a stone's throw of Green Point lighthouse. In a matter of hours she split just forward of the superstructure, and her cargo of Australian wool, destined for France, was washed up on the rocks and beaches. Fortunately there was no loss of life, the crew taking to the boats soon after dawn. Some days later the wreck caught fire and burned fiercely for about two weeks.

3 The 5 500-ton Russian trawler depot ship *Simferopol,* built in Leningrad in 1960, remains one of the few vessels to have escaped from the Skeleton Coast of South West Africa. She went aground near Walvis Bay in the early 1960s but was salvaged by tugs.

4 The 210 000 d.w.t. Shell tanker *Mactra* was sailing in ballast near Beira when a massive explosion ripped open nearly 130

metres of deck plating. The resulting fire took ten hours to subdue, and the final casualties were two dead and eight seriously injured. The stricken vessel was able to steam towards Beira under her own power, but for the tow to Durban four salvage tugs were in attendance. On 14 January 1970 she became the largest vessel to enter

Durban harbour, where temporary repairs were done, using about 1 700 tons of steel. After spending over six months in the harbour she was escorted by the tug *Atlantic* to Japan for permanent repairs.

5 The Victory ship *Hongkong Grace*, owned by C.Y. Tung, was involved in a collision with the tanker *Mina* off Mossel Bay in

May 1973. After temporary repairs she continued her voyage.

6 Two Liberian tankers collided off Cape Agulhas in August 1972: the ballasted *Texanita* sank following an explosion, but the *Oswego Guardian* proceeded under her own power to Cape Town, where she underwent temporary repairs.

1 The Irvin and Johnson trawler *Bluff* was one of four similar vessels built for the Cape Town fishing concern in 1934/5. On 15 September 1939 she was commissioned as a minesweeper for the Seaward Defence Force, taking the number T21. She resumed her peacetime role in 1944 and served the company for another twenty-two years. Her end came on 30 January 1966 when she ran ashore near Bakoven, Camps Bay.

2 The immense power of the sea is illustrated by this overturned bow section of a whaler wrecked on Dassen Island, off the West Coast. Probably the most famous ship to be lost near Dassen Island was the record-breaking first *Windsor Castle,* one of Donald Currie's flyers of the 1870s. In 1873 she had reduced the passage from England to the Cape to 23 days. In October 1876, southbound, she struck a reef off Dassen Island during the night and become a total loss.

In July 1971 the collision of the Unicorn coasters *Ovambo* and *Zulu* further up the West Coast near Cape Columbine caused the sinking of the latter.

More recently, in March 1978, the year-old Greek-owned bulk carrier *Pantelis A. Lemos* was lost along the West Coast at Vondeling Island on the Langebaan Peninsula. Grave negligence by the navigating officer on duty was responsible for this casualty.

3 The winter months of July and August in 1974 produced a spate of casualties in South African waters, reminiscent of the last century. On 10 August the Norwegian tanker *Produce,* outward bound from Durban, struck the notorious Aliwal Shoal near Umkomaas and sank shortly afterwards. The modern cargo liner *S.A. Oranjeland,* built in 1969 for South African Lines, rescued twenty-one survivors from the tanker and headed for East London, where she disembarked the survivors and loaded cargo for Europe. On 13 August she sailed from East London, but immediately after dropping the pilot she had a complete engine breakdown and drifted ashore in a remarkably short time just outside the harbour entrance. After several unsuccessful efforts to tow her off she was declared a total loss.

4 Slangkop at Kommetjie, on the west coast of the Cape Peninsula, first became widely known in 1910 when a radio station was established there. After the *Maori* was wrecked at Duiker Point in August 1909, and the Bullard King liner *Umhlali* became a total loss some distance to the south of Kommetjie only six weeks later, moves were set afoot to have a lighthouse erected. However, another ten years passed before Slangkop light was seen by mariners navigating near the Peninsula.

5 On a fine November afternoon in Table Bay in 1970 the Kuwaiti

tanker *Kazimah* was lying in ballast off Robben Island. There was an apparent total loss of power on board, preventing the anchors from being dropped. Tug aid was summoned, but by the time it arrived the *Kazimah* had drifted aground on the north-west corner of the island. Salvage experts and divers assessed the damage and it was found that several tanks were open to the sea. Fuel oil was pumped ashore and compressed air forced into the tanks. The German tug *Atlantic* and several harbour tugs, including the *T.S. McEwen,* joined forces in a towing attempt. Weather conditions remained favourable, and during spring tide on 29 November the *Kazimah* was refloated. With the 45-year-old *T.S. McEwen* towing proudly, assisted by the *F.T. Bates* and the *T.H. Watermeyer,* the tanker was brought into the harbour later that day.

1, 2, 3 The smart coaster *Horizon*, built in 1954, was acquired by African Coasters in 1964. She was used on the Durban to Cape Town run and also made trips to Mauritius. In May 1967, while on an inshore course to Durban, she ran aground at full speed near Cape Hermes south of Port St Johns on the Transkei coast. The crew were able to launch the lifeboats and head for the open sea, where a ship had been standing by during the night. Although the almost sheer cliff made salvage a difficult undertaking, some cargo was retrieved. The pounding of the waves soon broke the *Horizon* into several sections and she had to be written off as a total loss.

4 From September 1968 this Greek freighter, the *Alexfan,* was part of the harbour scene in Durban for nearly two years. Plagued by fire in her holds, engine failure, her owner's financial problems and attachment orders against her, she spent most of her time at buoys near the Esplanade. Her condition deteriorated steadily, and in 1970 she was sold for scrap.

5, 6 1 July 1966 was a typical midwinter's day in Table Bay, with a gale force north-wester bringing driving rain and heavy seas to the harbour approaches. Residents living near the sea front at Mouille Point and Sea Point were already aware of the disaster that had taken place during the night. The cargo liner *S.A. Seafarer* had arrived off the port with a full load of general cargo from England and the Continent. Owing to the poor weather conditions the port authorities had instructed the

captain to keep well clear of the harbour, as his ship would only be able to dock at dawn, but he had nevertheless decided to make an approach and proceed to an anchorage. During the approach the ship had gone off course as a result of the wind, the current and negligent navigation, and had hit the rocks close to Green Point lighthouse shortly after midnight. She had broken her back before sunrise, when three helicopters lifted the twelve passengers and sixty-four crew to safety. Heavy breakers, caused by a succession of winter gales, later ripped the hull into three sections.

1 The third major shipping
disaster to occur along the South
African seaboard in 1974 was the
loss of the 59 000 d.w.t. Liberian-
registered bulk-carrier *Oriental
Pioneer*. Heavy weather off the
east coast caused the vessel to
develop a list and a leak. Fearing
that a shift in her cargo of iron
ore would capsize her, the
captain decided to take his ship
into shallow water. His position
was some miles east of Cape
Agulhas when the order was
given to turn to starboard.
Shortly after this the vessel
became firmly wedged on a reef
about 1 kilometre off Struis Bay.
For a month efforts were made to
refloat her, but on 22 August she
showed signs of breaking up and
her crew were taken off.

2 The remains of the 250-ton
whaler *Stellenberg* at Saldanha
Bay. She had been a unit of the
South African Mine Clearance
Flotilla during the Second World
War and had taken part in
Operation Bellringer, during
which five Vichy-French ships
were captured south-east of Port
Elizabeth.

3 Japanese and Taiwanese
fishing vessels have operated in
South African waters for more
than two decades, and in that
period about forty have either
run aground, sunk at sea, or been
towed back to port with engine
problems. The photograph shows
a Taiwanese tuna boat aground
at Oyster Bay in the Eastern
Cape.

4 The *Siroco-1*, previously the
Mayflower X, spent some years
carrying coal from Maputo to
Cape ports on charter to South

African Railways. On 4 March
1976 she collided with a
breakwater in Table Bay,
resulting in damage costing
R500 000.

5 A rather small Japanese tug,
the *Kiyo Maru 2*, had been given
the difficult task of towing two
derelict tankers from Greece to
the shipbreakers' yards in
Taiwan, using the Cape route in
midwinter. Weather conditions
worsened as the tow approached
Table Bay on 28 July 1977, and
harbour authorities warned the
tug captain to remain well clear.
Whilst turning away, the towline
parted and the *Antipolis* (seen
here) drifted for some hours
before grounding at Oudekraal.
A similar fate awaited the second
tanker, the *Romelia*, which
broke free later during the night
and was wrecked on the rocks at
Llandudno.

4

5

THE WOODEN jetties, the small-craft basins, the tug moorings – for many people these are the most interesting and colourful places in our harbours, providing scenes of great activity and endless variety. Not so long ago, in a quieter corner, you would have found whalers moored for the winter, waiting to resume their work in Antarctic waters. These ships have now disappeared, but there are still the trawlers, the tugs and the dredgers, whose functional appearance is so different from that of earlier vessels, which had tall, raked funnels that spewed clouds of smoke from coal-fired machinery. Although modern technology has altered the appearance and characteristics of smaller craft, and thereby done much to change the atmosphere of our harbours, the corners of dockland from which these vessels operate continue to be a source of irrestistible fascination ■

1 The *A.J. Termorshuizen*, which belongs to a new class of

CHAPTER VIII
MARITIME MISCELLANY

pilot launch being used in South African harbours.

2 The East London harbour tug *F. Schermbrucker* in the port's Princess Elizabeth Dry Dock, which was opened by Princess Elizabeth during the royal tour of South Africa in 1947. This tug had the misfortune to be holed while assisting a freighter into port in 1963. She immediately headed towards shallow water where she sank. Naval salvage teams raised her and she resumed service some months later.

3 The harbours at Richard's Bay, Durban, East London and Walvis Bay require constant dredging. Seen here is one of Durban's older dredgers, whose familiar clank and grind will disappear as these craft are replaced by modern vessels.

OFF THE WEST coast of
Southern Africa flows the
Benguela Current,
bringing cold water northwards
from the Southern Ocean. This
current provides ideal conditions
for the growth of phytoplankton,
the basic food of pelagic fish such
as pilchards and anchovy. These
fish, in turn, attract seals and
millions of seabirds, a fact noted
by the early governors of the
Cape, who sent expeditions along
the coast to hunt the seals for
their pelts and flesh and also to
collect birds' eggs to augment the
protein supply of the settlement.
Later, hundreds of vessels came
to the coast to transport 'white
gold' (guano) to Europe for use as
agricultural fertilizer.

However, it was the fish that
led to the establishment of a
more lasting industry. Early
paintings and sketches, such as
those of Thomas Bowler, show
Malays, wearing their pointed
straw hats, fishing from tiny
craft off Cape Town. Further up

the coast, fishing villages grew in many coves and paved the way for the fish canneries, fish-meal plants and crayfish processing factories of today.

The first steam trawler started operating off the Cape just before the turn of the century. In 1910, the two main trawling concerns merged their interests to form Irvin and Johnson, whose fleet still trawls the seas. Today, however, the sophisticated ships of Irvin and Johnson, Atlantic Trawling, and other operators, bear no resemblance to the coal-burning vessels of only two decades ago.

A number of Asian countries have been forced, through rapid population growth, to exploit every available source of protein, and among other things they have looked to the fishing grounds of the West Coast and the Agulhas Bank. In the early 1960s Japanese stern trawlers came this way, followed by vessels from Taiwan, Korea and other countries in the Far East. These, and long-line tuna catchers, transship their cargoes to refrigerated vessels for the long passage home. Many of these fishing craft have been overwhelmed by heavy seas and wrecked along our shores ■

1 The 'snoekers' of the Cape in 1935. During subsequent harbour works this area, Roggebaai, was covered by millions of cubic metres of soil to form part of Cape Town's 'Foreshore' area. The Random Mole, built in 1932, is also visible.
2 The *Afrikander,* like most South African trawlers over the years, was of British design.
3 In the light of modern automation in the fishing industry this scene looks archaic, yet the photograph was taken only twenty years ago.
4 The *Blomvlei,* one of Irvin and Johnson's coal-burning trawlers. She did anti-submarine patrols off the coast during the Second World War.
5 One of the last South African coal-burning trawlers, the *Grootvlei.* In 1970 she was scuttled in Table Bay to create an artificial reef for fish breeding.
6 The diesel-powered *Erica,* a latterday side trawler.
7 The *Aloe,* one of the more recent stern trawlers, digs in south of Cape Point.

1

2

FOR THE WHALING season from November to April, great fleets of whalers with their factory ships headed 'down south' into Antarctic waters, a phenomenon which continued until the mid-1960s. Dutch, Norwegian, British and (for a time) American ships were involved. They would arrive in Table Bay within a few days of each other, the factory ships entering harbour immediately and the catchers berthing at intervals. Cape Town became a 'halfway house' at which fresh provisions, stores and fuel were taken aboard for the long sojourn in the Antarctic. Some South Africans obtained employment on these vessels as labourers, galley boys, or what have you, and gained interesting experiences in a region of the world where few had ventured.

The almost indiscriminate catching of whales led to

3

4

increasing pressure against the slaughter of endangered species. As a result the fleets dwindled and international whaling operations have now ceased almost completely ■

1 The 'fishbag' is hauled aboard a stern trawler via the slipway. The different method of trawling used today has led to a radical alteration in trawler design. The bridge, which has 360-degree visibility, is situated as far forward as possible, and the fish deck is now aft of the superstructure to allow for the stern ramp. Today's trawlers have machinery to process the fish and refrigerate the holds (in contrast to earlier vessels, which used blocks of ice to keep the fish cool).

2 Trawlers at Table Bay harbour's South Arm. These vessels are the size of some regular liners of the last century.

3 Unloading fish by hand before the era of total automation.

4 Whalers refitting in Durban in 1934.

5 The whale factory ships *Kosmos IV*, *Pelagos* and *Norhval* in Table Bay harbour in April 1949 after the whaling season. While homeward bound, a previous *Kosmos* was sunk in 1940 by the German raider *Thor*, and over 18 000 tons of whale oil was lost. In another action against whalers, this time in the Southern Ocean by the raider *Pinguin*, two factory ships, a supply tanker and nine whalers were captured in January 1941.

6 The *Balaena* heads south in November 1948. She was withdrawn in the early 1960s and was the last of the British factory ships to pass this way.

7 The South African-operated factory ship *Tafelberg*, which went to the Antarctic whaling grounds for Irvin and Johnson in the 1930s. She was lost during the Second World War while carrying oil on behalf of the Admiralty.

5

6

7

WHALING IN South African waters began as early as the seventeenth century, when whalermen, using hand-held harpoons, hunted their prey from small cutters in False Bay. Other places – Saldanha Bay, Betty's Bay, Plettenberg Bay, and more – have served as whaling stations over the years. It was a tight-rope existence, and some companies folded up before catching their first whale. Local whaling activities have now ceased completely ■

1 Ysterfontein on the West Coast is one of South Africa's 'ghost' whaling stations. Saldanha, further north, was the base for a number of Norwegian whalers which operated in local waters.

2 The biggest whale factory ship to call here was the Dutch vessel *Willem Barendsz,* built in 1959. She became a South African 'fish factory ship' after only fifteen whaling trips to the Antarctic. When the fishing industry

slumped in the early 1970s she was disposed of. The fish factory ship *Suiderkruis*, also a converted whale factory ship, suffered a similar fate.

3 The *Uni-2* was involved in whaling along the South African coast.

4 In the heyday of Antarctic whaling, many whalers spent the winter months in South African ports. As a result of the decline in whaling, scores of whalers were scrapped. An indication of the decline is the fact that only ten whalers are shown in this photograph, which was taken in Table Bay harbour in 1964. In the foreground are two vessels powered by gas turbines.

5 The whale slipway in Durban in 1962. This was the last active whaling station in South Africa.

UNTIL THE 1970s South African tugs were designed for two purposes: to assist ships into and out of harbours, and to act as salvage vessels. They were advanced craft for their time, having navigational, salvage and radio equipment of the highest standards.

The *Ludwig Wiener,* which came out in 1913, was the first tug of any significance ordered by the South African Railways and Harbours Administration. (Previous tugs were either privately owned or operated by colonial Governments.) A building programme from 1934 to 1954 added eleven large coal-burning tugs to the harbour service. In 1950 two large oil-burners made their appearance, and three more similar vessels arrived between 1959 and 1961, the third of these, the *J.R. More,* being the last steam tug ordered for South African harbours ∎

1 A tug-master in 1956.
2 On coal-burning tugs considerable effort was required from the stokers. A loss of steam at a crucial moment could endanger not only the tug but also the ship she was attending. A Durban tug on a salvage mission suffered the indignity of having to be towed in because the stokers had become seasick

and an adequate head of steam could not be maintained!

3 Built in 1925 in answer to the need for powerful tugs to handle the large mailships of the time, the *T.S. McEwen* originally had tall masts, the foremast being ahead of the bridge. When ships with flared bows and aircraft carriers came on the scene, her tug-master had to be careful not to lose the foremast. As the salvage tug which attended many of the marine casualties along the coast, she became famous. Her last such mission was to assist in refloating the tanker *Kazimah* from the rocks on Robben Island. Instead of becoming the show-piece at a maritime museum, she suffered an ignominious fate when she was scuttled in 1977.

4 Ordered for the Natal government in 1902, the *Harry Escombe* was one of the early dual-purpose tugs on the seaboard. She did service, including some remarkable salvage tows, until 1953, when she was stripped and used for naval gunnery practice.

5 The builder's plate on the tug *T.H. Watermeyer*.

6 Fire-fighting equipment aboard the *Danie Hugo* is demonstrated at the final departure of the *S.A. Oranje* from Table Bay harbour in 1975.

1 The Durban tug *Sir William Hoy* saw 51 years' service in the port. Her coal-fired reciprocating triple expansion engines produced a towing capacity equal to that of any other South African harbour tug. She was scrapped in 1979.

2 Built in 1954, the coal-burning, twin-screw *R.B. Waterston* (left) contrasts strongly with the Voith-Schneider-propelled *J.H. Botha,* built in 1974. The former tug represents the propulsion type used in South African harbours for more than a century.

3 The *T.H. Watermeyer* was one of eleven coal-burning harbour tugs built between 1934 and 1954 for the South African Railways and Harbours Administration. All had salvage and fire-fighting gear, as well as equipment for harbour work. The last coal-burner in service, the *J.D. White,* was withdrawn in 1980.

4 The *F.C. Sturrock*, the tripod-masted *J.R. More*, and the *Danie Hugo* (shown here) represent the final chapter in South African steam tugs. They had very pleasant lines and were probably the best-proportioned tugs in the world.

5 The *E.S. Steytler* had an interesting history. Like the *T.H. Watermeyer,* her delivery was delayed by the Second World War. Her original name, *Theodore Woker,* had to be changed because of its German connotations. Just after the war she sank after being holed by one of the propellers of the Cunarder *Georgic* in Durban harbour. She was refloated and repaired, and continued in service, mainly at East London, until she was withdrawn in 1980.

WHEN the steam tugs (particularly the coal-burners) started becoming obsolete, other tug types were investigated. The Voith-Schneider propulsion system, which allows the tug to move (and therefore push or pull) in any direction instantly, was found most suitable for harbour work. A tug replacement programme therefore began in 1974 with the building of vessels of this design. The salvage function of harbour tugs had passed to the specialized salvage tugs of Safmarine, and of Land and Marine and Salvage Contractors.

Apart from two French-built vessels and three from Japanese yards, all the harbour tugs are locally built. They are mostly of the Voith-Schneider design, but there are also Schottel, Z-peller and controllable-pitch Diesel Kort rudder propulsion systems. Because of their degree of manoeuvrability these tugs are a vast improvement on the steam tugs, which were powerful but not entirely suited to harbour work. Whereas the bulk and sluggish movement of the earlier tugs made ship handling rather difficult in bad weather, the new vessels are extremely functional ∎

1 A steam pilot tug of 1958 vintage. In 1983 the last three vessels of this type were bought by Australians, who attempted to sail them home. However, they were laid up in South African ports and will probably be scrapped here.
2 The *T. Eriksen*, another of the vessels built between 1934 and 1954. She also sank after being holed by a ship's propeller in Durban, and was later refloated.
3 The *Danie du Plessis* (shown here) and her sister ship, the *Willem Heckroodt*, were the first diesel-electric tugs to be built in South Africa (1969).
4 The first Voith-Schneider tug in Cape Town, the *J.H. Botha*, picks up the towing wire.
5 One of the locally-built pilot launches, the *H.T.V. Horner*, off East London
6 The *W.H. Andrag* is one of the latest Voith-Schneider tugs. All-round visibility from the bridge is an outstanding feature. These vessels also have a towing engine, which assists greatly when prolonged towing is necessary.

1 Scientific research into various aspects of the fishing industry has been in progress for a number of years. The research ship *Africana* is the third vessel to bear this name since the Second World War. She was built in Durban yards in 1981 and has the most modern equipment for research.

2 When the tanker *Wafra* grounded at Cape Agulhas in 1971, causing extensive coastal pollution, the South African tugs dispatched to the scene tried in vain to salvage her. Their power, though more than adequate in previous decades, did not match the increased size of tankers. The powerful German tug *Oceanic* managed to refloat the *Wafra,* and towed her out to sea to be sunk by Air Force planes.

In response to the obvious need for specialist local salvage tugs,

Safmarine ordered two 26 000 i.h.p. vessels capable of 21 knots and a towing pull of 205 tonnes. These vessels, the *S.A. Wolraad Woltemade* and the *S.A. John Ross* (shown here), have carried out a number of spectacular salvage operations, such as that associated with the burning tanker *Castillo de Bellver* off the West Coast in 1983. There have

also been some rather interesting deep-sea tows, including a number through the treacherous Chilean Archipelago and the Straits of Magellan. Salvage tugs are also operated by Land and Marine and Salvage Contractors of Cape Town, whose tugs, although smaller than those of Safmarine, have rendered valuable service.

With tugs of this capacity around, modern harbour tugs are no longer dual-purpose vessels but have been designed solely to fulfill their harbour functions.

3 To transport men and equipment to the scientific bases in Antarctica and on Marion Island, as well as to the meteorological station on Gough Island, a special supply and research ship, the *RSA*, was built in Japan in 1961. She is seen here on her maiden voyage.

4 The *S.A. Agulhas* replaced the *RSA* in 1978. She is a larger vessel with many more facilities. Her predecessor is now a

training ship for seamen and is moored in Table Bay harbour.
5 Occasionally the undersea cable connecting South Africa with Europe is damaged, either by natural causes or by a trawl net. On station is a cable ship specially equipped to repair the cable. Seen here in Table Bay harbour is the *Mercury*, a vessel which is similar to but more modern than the South African cable ship *Cable Restorer*.
6 The recent search for oil under the continental shelf has so far yielded potential for a gasfield about 100 kilometres off Mossel Bay. To service the offshore drilling rigs, Unicorn Lines ordered the *Voortrekker* from Durban yards.

1 Research work aboard the *S.A. Agulhas*. Recent programmes have included research on krill, a major source of food for some species of whale and other marine creatures.

2 Crossing the Antarctic Circle for the first time requires an initiation ceremony, with King Neptune in his polar outfit. The gist of the ceremony is that the newcomers get plastered with such things as raw eggs. But, like the ceremony for Crossing the Line, it can be fun – to watch!

3 The Roaring Forties begin only a few hours south of Cape Town. On nearly every voyage to Antarctica or the islands, the *S.A. Agulhas* has to plough through mountainous seas, whipped to a frenzy by force 10 to 12 gales. Visibility is often down to zero because of rain, fog or even blizzards. The further south the ship, the more frequent are the iceberg sightings.

4 Preparing to launch Unicorn Lines' container ship *Berg* at Durban in 1977.

5 The steel trawler *Afrikaner* being launched from the Globe Shipyard in Table Bay harbour in 1970. A shortage of space made the 'sideways launch' necessary.

ORGANIZED SHIPBUILDING began in South Africa during the rule of the Dutch East India Company, when small wooden vessels were built. Even in more recent times, only wooden fishing craft and the occasional small steel tug took to the water from local shipyards. Knysna was one of the ports where shipbuilding took place, the nearby forests yielding the necessary timber. In addition to fishing boats and pleasure craft, a few motor patrol launches came from Knysna yards during the Second World War. From the late 1950s steel trawlers, harbour craft and various research vessels were launched from the Globe Shipyard in Cape Town. However, with two major shipyards Durban has become the country's main shipbuilding port, producing most of the recent harbour tugs, ten coasters for Unicorn Lines, and a variety of other ships, including sophisticated vessels for the South African Navy. Recent announcements indicate that submarines and other naval vessels will also be built at these yards. With the apparently viable gasfield off Mossel Bay, the building of rig tenders will probably occur. Future orders from foreign countries for both merchant and naval ships are also possible ■

DURING THE Second World War ship repairers in South Africa undertook the conversion of regular vessels to armed merchant cruisers, troopships or minesweepers. They also repaired ships damaged in action or by mines, and they degaussed northbound vessels. These activities gave the industry an international reputation, confirmed by the fact that numerous major refitting or repair contracts (such as those on the *Aimee Lykes,* the *Mactra,* and the *Kazimah*) have subsequently been awarded to local concerns.

During the Suez closures the increased volume of traffic yielded many clients and the industry boomed. In recent years, however, a decrease in the number of ships passing through local waters has led to a decline in the ship repair industry, but the potential of the yards remains an important strategic factor in South African maritime affairs ■

1 Table Bay harbour's Sturrock Dry Dock. With a docking length of 360 metres, this is the longest dry dock on the coast. Also in Table Bay harbour is the smaller Robinson Dry Dock. The Prince Edward Dry Dock in Durban, the Princess Elizabeth Dry Dock in East London and Simonstown's Selborne Dry Dock are the only other facilities for under-water work on larger ships. Floating docks and slipways are generally used for smaller vessels.

Unfortunately the dry docks were built to accommodate the relatively narrow hulls of the liners and warships of the time. While the docking length in the Sturrock and Prince Edward Dry Docks is adequate for today's tankers, the width presents a problem. Underwater work on these giant vessels must therefore be done elsewhere.
2 Maintenance work during the

3

scheduled dry docking of a large container ship.

3 Sunset at Doringbaai, a typical West Coast fishing village where the pace of life is leisurely but where fishermen still face the perils of the sea. It was here that a fishing boat capsized in 1970 with the loss of seventeen lives.

4 Morning fog over the lagoon at Langebaan. Saldanha Bay, with its iron-ore terminal, stands at the northern end of this magnificent stretch of water which has seen the changing face of South African maritime affairs. It witnessed the first recorded naval engagement in South African waters, and its port has grown from a tranquil fishing village to become the most important harbour on the African continent for exporting iron ore.

4

Bibliography

Bock, K. and B. *Die roten Handelsflotten*, Koehler, Herford, 1977.

Burman, J. *Bay of Storms*, Human and Rousseau, Cape Town, 1976. *Great Shipwrecks off the Coast of Southern Africa*, C. Struik, Cape Town, 1967. *Strange Shipwrecks*, C. Struik, Cape Town, 1968.

Cape of Good Hope and Port Natal Shipping and Mercantile Gazette, 1844-1861, weekly.

Coles, A. *Merchant Ships, World Built*, Adlard Coles, Southampton, annual.

Denfield, J. *Pioneer Port*, Howard Timmins, Cape Town, 1965.

Dunn, L. *British Passenger Liners*, Adlard Coles, Southampton, 1959. *Passenger Liners*, Adlard Coles, London, 1965. *The World's Tankers*, Adlard Coles, London, 1956.

Du Toit, A.K. *Ships of the South African Navy*, S.A. Boating Publications, Cape Town, 1976.

Frank, W. *The Sea Wolves*, Weidenfeld and Nicolson, London, 1955.

Goosen, J.C. *South Africa's Navy – The First Fifty Years*, Flesch, Cape Town, 1973.

Green, L. *A Giant in Hiding*, Howard Timmins, Cape Town, 1970. *At Daybreak for the Isles*, Howard Timmins, Cape Town, 1950. *Eight Bells at Salamander*, Howard Timmins, Cape Town, 1960. *Harbours of Memory*, Howard Timmins, Cape Town, 1969. *South African Beachcomber*, Howard Timmins, Cape Town, 1958. *Tavern of the Seas*, Howard Timmins, Cape Town, 1947. *Where Men still Dream*, Howard Timmins, Cape Town, 1949.

Hansen, H.J. *Die Schiffe der deutschen Flotten 1848-1945*, Stalling, Oldenburg, 1973.

Harris, J. *Without Trace*, Eyre Methuen, London, 1981.

Hart, G.H.T. *A Historical Geography of Port Natal*, unpublished M.A. thesis, University of the Witwatersrand, 1966.

Hocking, C. *Dictionary of Disasters at Sea during the Age of Steam*, Lloyds, London, 1969.

Hughes, D. *Cruise Liners to the Cape*, Downstairs Graphics, Pretoria, 1984.

Hughes, D. and Humphries, P. *In South African Waters*, Oxford University Press, Cape Town, 1977.

Industrial Publishing Corporation *Ports of South Africa*, IPC, Florida, annual.

Ingpen, B.D. *South African Merchant Ships*, A.A. Balkema, Cape Town, 1979. *The Coastwise Shipping Industry of Southern Africa*, unpublished M.A. thesis, University of Port Elizabeth, 1983.

Kemp, P. (ed.) *The Oxford Companion to Ships and the Sea*, Oxford University Press and Granada, London, 1976.

Kennedy, R.F. *Shipwrecks on and off the Coasts of Southern Africa*, Johannesburg Public Library, 1955.

Kludas, A. *Die grossen Passagierschiffe der Welt* (Vol. 1-5), Stalling, Oldenburg/Hamburg, 1972-74. *Die grossen Passagierschiffe Fähren und Cruise Liner der Welt*, Koehler, Herford, 1983. *Die Schiffe der deutsche Afrika-Linien, 1880-1945*, Stalling, Hamburg, 1975.

Lloyds Register of Shipping, Lloyds, London, annual.

Martin, H.J. and Orpen, N. *South Africa at War*, Purnell, Cape Town, 1979.

Marsh, J.H. *No Pathway Here*, Howard Timmins, Cape Town, 1948. *Skeleton Coast*, Hodder and Stoughton, Cape Town and London, 1944.

Murray, M. *Ships and South Africa*, Oxford University Press, London, 1935. *The Union-Castle Chronicle*, Longmans, London, 1953.

Osborn, R.F. *C.G. – A Great Natalian*, C.G. Smith and Co., Durban, 1966.

Pollock, N.P. and Agnew, S. *A Historical Geography of South Africa*, Longmans, London, 1963.

Report of the Committee of Inquiry in Connection with the Shipping Service Operated by the Railways and Harbours Administration, Government Printer, Pretoria, 1952.

Reynolds, D. *A Century of South African Steam Tugs*, Downstairs Graphics, Pretoria, 1981.

Rogge, B. and Frank, W. *Schiff 16*, Stalling, Oldenburg, 1955.

Rowe, J. and Crabtree, A. *Shipwrecks of the Southern Cape*, Atlantic Underwater Club, Cape Town, 1978.

Shaffer, N.M. *The Competitive Position of the Port of Durban*, North Western University, Evanston, 1965.

Sharp, P. *Outwards from Port Natal*, Tafelberg, Cape Town, 1978. *Pilot*, T.V. Bulpin, Cape Town, 1972. *Tales of Table Bay*, T.V. Bulpin, Cape Town, 1975.

Ship Society of South Africa *Flotsam and Jetsam*, Cape Town, quarterly.

Solomon, V.E. *The South African Shipping Question, 1886-1914*, Historical Publishing Society, Cape Town, 1982.

South African Department of Foreign Affairs and Information *South Africa 1983 – The Official Yearbook of the Republic of South Africa*, Johannesburg, Chris van Rensburg, 1983.

South African Marine Corporation Ltd *The Wheelhouse*, Cape Town, quarterly.

South African Navy *Navy News*, Simonstown, monthly.

South African Shipping Commission *Interim Report* (1945), *Final Report* (1947), Cape Town.

South African Transport Services *Harbour News*, Johannesburg, monthly.

South African Transport Services *African Harbours*, S.A.T.S., Johannesburg, 1982.

South African Transport, Bolton Publications, Johannesburg, monthly.

Standard Encyclopaedia of Southern Africa, 12 volumes, Nasou, Cape Town, 1971.

Storrar, P. *Portrait of Plettenberg Bay*, Centaur, Cape Town, 1978.

Stuttaford, M. (ed.) *Port Services Guide: Cape Sea Route*, Thomson Publications, Cape Town, 1982.

Stuttaford, M. (ed.) *South African Shipping News and Fishing Industry Review*, M. Stuttaford, Stellenbosch, monthly.

Thomson Publications *A Century of Service*, Thomson Publications, Cape Town, 1983.

Turner, L.C.F., et al *War in the Southern Oceans*, Oxford University Press, Cape Town, 1961.

Unicorn Lines *New Frontiers*, Durban, quarterly.

Van Delden, G. *I Have a Plan*, Howard Timmins, Cape Town, 1950.

Verburgh, C. *Ontwikkeling en Vooruitsigte van die Suid-Afrikaanse Handelsvloot*, Weaver, Stellenbosch, 1966.

Wexham, B. *Shipwrecks of the Western Cape*, Howard Timmins, Cape Town, 1983.

Wiese, B. *Seaports and Port Cities of Southern Africa*, Steiner, Wiesbaden, 1981.

Young, G. *Farewell to the Tramps*, Midgley, Kommetjie, 1982. *Salt in my Blood*, Midgley, Kommetjie, 1975. *Ships that Pass*, Midgley, Kommetjie, 1976.

Newspapers
Cape Times, Cape Town, daily.
The Argus, Cape Town, daily.
The Daily News, Durban, daily.
The Eastern Province Herald, Port Elizabeth, daily.

Photographic Credits

(Photograph numbers are in italic type, page numbers in roman type.)

Peter Bilas (paintings): *3*, 8/*2*, 46/*2*, 98-99.
Bredasdorp Museum: 28/*2*.
Bundesarchiv, Koblenz: 59/*5*.
Cape Archives (archival references in brackets): 11/*2* (J1679), 20/*1* (AG11688), 23/*7* (AG5373), 24/*1* (E8211), 26/*2* (E8202), 28/*1* (M774), 29/*4* (AG7145), 30/*2* (AG13580), 31/*4* (J1392), 32/*4* (E2080), 34/*1* (AG13682), 37/*3* (AG1230), 38/*3* (AG189), 39/*6* (AG190), 47/*3* (AG13672), 48/*2* (J1533), 48/*3* (E8575), 48/*4* (E9342), 51/*4* (R1112), 72/*1* (AG3953), 76/*1* (E8661), 78/*1* (E8648), 80/*1* (AG3111), 81/*4* (AG3207), 103/*3* (AG3186), 138-139 (M746), 140/*2* (E8658), 141/*4* (J8086), 141/*5* (M519), 142/*4* (AG13420), 158/*4* (E8600).
Dr E.M. Cornish: 13/*2* (and Mrs V. Barry), 15/*4*, 62/*3* (and Mrs V. Barry), 65/*5*, 82/*1* (and Mrs V. Barry), 83/*2* (and Mrs V. Barry), 83/*3* (and Mrs V. Barry), 83/*4* (and Mrs V. Barry), 85/*3* (and Mrs V. Barry), 91/*4* (and Mrs V. Barry), 92/*1* (and Mrs V. Barry), 92/*2* (and Mrs V. Barry), 109/*5*, 110/*2* (and A. Duncan), 112/*2*, 118/*4*, 119/*5*, 122/*1*, 125/*6*, 143/*5*, 146/*1*, 146/*2*, 146/*4*, 147/*5*, 147/*6*, 148/*3*, 151/*4*, 151/*6*, 152/*2*, 154/*2*, 154/*3*, 157/*6*, 164/*1*, 165/*5*, 166/*2*, 168/*2*, 169/*4*.
Clyde Davidson: 42/*2*, 86/*2*, 88/*3*, 90/*3*.
Deutsches Schiffahrtsmuseum, Bremerhaven (Arnold Kludas): 52/*1*, 52/*2*.
A. Duncan: 121/*4*, 121/*5*.
Raymond Hancock: *1*, 18/*1*, 36/*2*, 123/*5*, 128/*2*, 129/*5*, 150/*1*, 150/*2*, 150/*3*.
H.E. Healing (prints from Capt. C.J. Harris collection): 57/*5*, 65/*4*, 66/*1*, 103/*4*, 104/*1*.

Eric Hoskings: 15/*3*, 87/*3*, 87/*4*, 87/*5*, 88/*1*.
Brian Ingpen: *2*, *4*, 8/*1*, 11/*3*, 12/*1*, 13/*3*, 22/*2*, 23/*3*, 24/*2*, 24/*3*, 27/*2*, 29/*5*, 30/*1*, 32/*3*, 33/*5*, 36/*1*, 40/*2*, 41/*5*, 42/*1*, 43/*4*, 43/*5*, 71/*4*, 91/*5*, 96/*2*, 97/*5*, 117/*6*, 117/*7*, 118/*2*, 126/*1*, 126/*2*, 126/*3*, 127/*6*, 127/*7*, 128/*1*, 149/*4*, 154/*1*, 158/*2*, 160/*1*, 164/*2*, 165/*4*, 166/*3*, 166/*4*, 167/*6*, 172/*1*, 172/*3*, 173/*4*.
Irvin and Johnson: 156/*3*, 157/*7*, 158/*1*.
Werner Kaufmann: 63/*5*, 63/*6*, 70/*1*, 72/*2*, 96/*1*, 124/*4*, 134/*2*, 148/*1*, 151/*5*.
Local History Museum, Durban: 37/*4*, 38/*1*, 38/*2*, 39/*4*, 39/*5*, 40/*1*, 41/*3*, 41/*4*, 54/*2*, 58/*1*.
Maritime Museum, Cape Town: 46/*1*, 55/*4*, 55/*5*, 56/*1*, 56/*3* (and Miss E. May), 57/*7*, 58/*2*, 61/*4*, 61/*5*, 64/*2*.
Robert Pabst: 4-5, 14/*1*, 14/*2*, 16/*1*, 16/*2*, 16/*3*, 18/*2*, 23/*4*, 23/*5*, 26/*5*, 27/*4*, 30/*3*, 43/*3*, 44-45, 52/*3*, 61/*5*, 62/*4*, 66/*4*, 84/*1*, 84/*2*, 85/*4*, 86/*1*, 89/*5*, 90/*1*, 90/*2*, 91/*6*, 91/*7*, 92/*3*, 93/*4*, 93/*5*, 93/*6*, 94/*1*, 94/*2*, 96/*3*, 97/*4*, 97/*6*, 104/*2*, 104/*5*, 104/*6*, 105/*3*, 105/*4*, 106/*1*, 106/*2*, 106/*3*, 107/*5*, 108/*1*, 108/*2*, 109/*3*, 109/*4*, 111/*5*, 111/*6*, 113/*4*, 117/*8*, 118/*1*, 118/*3*, 119/*6*, 120/*1*, 122/*2*, 122/*4*, 124/*1*, 124/*3*, 130-131, 132/*1*, 132/*2*, 134/*1*, 134/*3*, 135/*4*, 136/*1*, 136/*2*, 137/*3*, 137/*4*, 145/*4*, 145/*5*, 149/*5*, 152/*1*, 153/*4*, 153/*5*, 156/*2*, 157/*4*, 157/*5*, 158/*3*, 160/*2*, 161/*3*, 161/*4*, 161/*5*, 162/*3*, 163/*5*, 163/*6*, 165/*3*, 166/*1*, 167/*5*, 168/*1*, 168/*3*, 169/*5*, 171/*5*.
Mrs M. Parkes: 28/*3*, 29/*6*.
Port Alfred Municipality (photography by Raymond Hancock): 32/*1*, 32/*2*.
Ship Society of South Africa (Martin Leendertz collection): 25/*4*, 26/*1*, 35/*3*, 35/*4*, 48/*1*, 49/*6*, 50/*1*, 53/*5*, 76/*2*, 77/*4*, 77/*5*, 78/*2*, 78/*3*, 78/*4*, 80/*2*, 80/*3*, 81/*5*, 100/*1*, 101/*2*, 101/*3*, 102/*1*, 102/*2*, 103/*5*, 105/*7*, 110/*3*, 121/*6*, 140/*1*, 142/*1*, 159/*7*, 162/*4*.
Simonstown Museum: 22/*6*, 47/*4*, 50/*2*, 51/*3*, 71/*3*.

South African Library: 74-75. Cape Times negative collection: 54/*1*, 58/*3*, 60/*1*, 60/*2*, 62/*2*, 71/*2*, 133/*3*, 133/*4*, 144/*2*, 156/*1*, 159/*5*, 159/*6*, 162/*1*, 162/*2*.
South African Marine Corporation Ltd: *6*, 88/*2*, 89/*4*, 112/*1*, 113/*3*, 114/*1*, 114/*2*, 114/*3*, 115/*4*, 115/*5*, 115/*6*, 116/*1*, 116/*2*, 116/*3*, 116/*4*, 116/*5*, 125/*5*, 126/*4*, 127/*5*, 129/*3*, 129/*4*, 172/*2*.
South African National Museum for Military History, Johannesburg: 49/*5*, 55/*3*, 56/*2*, 56/*4*, 57/*6*, 59/*4*, 64/*3*.
South African Transport Services (Publicity and Travel Department): 34/*2*, 110/*1*, 111/*4*.
South African Navy: 64/*1*, 66/*2*, 66/*3*, 67/*5*, 67/*6*, 67/*7*, 68/*1*, 68/*2*, 68/*3*, 69/*4*, 69/*5*.
State Archives, Windhoek (archival references in brackets): 20/*2*, (593), 21/*3* (6228), 62/*1* (1631), 77/*3* (2550), 142/*2* (4055), 142/*3* (1266), 145/*3* (635).
Professor L.G. Underhill: 10/*1*, 22/*1*, 31/*5*, 148/*2*, 152/*3*.
Unicorn Lines: 122/*3*, 124/*2*, 169/*6*, 171/*4*.
Rev. Don Williams: 170/*1*, 170/*2*, 170/*3*.

Whilst every effort has been made, the authors have been unable to trace the copyright owners of the following photographs and would appreciate any information that would enable them to do so: 53/*4* (print from Harris collection), 60/*3* (print from Harris collection), 78/*5* (print from Harris collection), 107/*4* (print from Pabst collection), 120/*2*, (print from Harris collection), 121/*3* (print from Hancock collection), 140/*3* (print from Hancock collection), 141/*6* (print from Hancock collection), 144/*1* (print from Hancock collection), 146/*3* (print from Pabst collection).

Index

(Bold numerals refer to captions of vessels illustrated.)

A.J. Termorshuizen **154**
Aberdeen White Star Line 140
Achille Lauro **135**
Adolf Woermann **77**
Adviser 59
Africa (1) (Italian liner) **92**
Africa (2) (container vessel) **118**
Africa Shell 123
African Coasters 121, 123, 145, 150
African Comet 26, **108**
African Crescent **109**
African Endeavor **93**
African Enterprise **93**
Africana **168**
Afrikander (Bucknall steamer) 106
Afrikander, HMS (R.N. base) 60
Afrikander (trawler) **157**
Afrikaner **170**
Agnar **28**
Agulhas 111
Aimee Lykes **109**, 172
Albion, HMS (aircraft carrier) 63
Alexfan **150**
Algoa Bay (*see also* Port Elizabeth
    harbour) 10, 31, 72
Almirante Saldanha 62
Aloe (1) **111**
Aloe (2) **111**
Aloe (stern trawler) **157**
Alpha see *Nolloth*
America (2) **136**
American South Africa Line *see*
    Mallory Transport Lines Inc.
Amphion, HMS **61**
Amra **57**
Anchises **89**
Andes (2) **97**
Andrew Weir and Company 107
Anglo-Boer War 48-50, *et passim*
Angola (2) **91**
Angra Pequena *see* Lüderitz
Antipolis **152**
Antrim, HMS (R.N. cruiser) 51
Apolda 110, **111**
Aquitania **54**, **55**
Armadale Castle 42, 83
Aronda 57
Arundel Castle (1) 80
Arundel Castle (2) **80**
Arundel Castle (3) 78, **81**, **87**
Aska 57
Astor 89, **95**
Asturias (2) **132**
Athlone Castle **14**, 82
Atlantic 147
Atlantis (German raider) **52**
Australia, HMAS **55**
Australis see *America* (2)
Bachante, HMS 9
Balaena **159**
Balmoral Castle (1) **83**
Barham, HMS 55
Barry, Joseph 28
Basuto Coast **144**
Beatty see *Howe*, HMS
Benoni, HMSAS **65**
Berg **170**
Biermann, Admiral H.H. 66, 71,
    123
Biermann, Rear-Admiral S.C. 66
Birkenhead, H.M. Paddle Steamer **47**
Bismarck 59
Blaauwberg, Battle of 47
Bloemfontein Castle 84
Blomvlei **157**
Blue Anchor Line 40, 142
Blue Funnel Line 89, 93, 95
Blue Star Line 117, 135, 144
Bluff **148**
Bluff, the (Durban) 10
Boissevain **14**, 79
Bosphorus (mail steamer) 100
Braemar Castle (1) **40**, **48**
Braemar Castle (3) 84
Brakpan, HMSAS **65**
Breede River 28, 121
British India Line 90

Brutus **140**
Bucknall Brothers (*see also*
    Ellerman and Bucknall) 11, 106,
Buffalo **123**
Buffalo River (*see also* East London
    harbour) 34, 37, 87
Bullard King (*see also* Kylsant
    Group) 49, 57, 79, 103, 149
Bulwark, HMS (aircraft carrier) 63
Cable Restorer 169
Cagni 132
Caltex Glasgow **125**
Calypso see *Southern Cross*
Canadian Pacific Line 58
Canberra **137**
Cape of Good Hope and West Coast
    of Africa Station 50
Cape Naval Volunteers 64
Cape Town see Table Bay harbour
Capetown Castle **14**, 58
Carnarvon, HMS (R.N. cruiser) 51
Carnarvon Castle (2) 14, **56-7**, 58,
    82, **85**, 87
Caronia **96**
Cassel **101**
Castillo de Bellver **168**
Castle Line (*see also* Union-Castle
    Line) 77
Cayzer, Irvine and Company (*see*
    also Clan Line) 104
Centaur 95
Ceramic 78
Chandris Lines 136-7
Chapman 72
Charente Steamship Company *see*
    Harrison Line
Christensen Canadian African
    Line 14
Chub **28**, **121**
City of Cambridge **49**
City of Cape Town **107**
City of Durban (1) **105**
City of Durban (2) **90**
City of Durban (3) 105-6, **119**
City of Exeter (2) **90**
City of Johannesburg **107**
City of Lincoln (1) 140, **142**
City of Lincoln (2) **146**
City of London (1) **79**
City of Melbourne see *City of Cape
    Town*
City of Port Elizabeth 90
City of Pretoria **107**
City of York 90
Clan Cumming **104**
Clan Farquhar **104**
Clan Graham **104**
Clan Lamont **104**
Clan Line (*see also* Cayzer, Irvine
    and Company) 103-5, 140
Clan Macintyre **142**
Clan MacIver **104**
Clan Monroe **140**
Clan Stuart **103**
Clara **29**
Cluny Castle (2) 103
Comrie Castle see *S.A. Vaal*
Companhia Nacional de Nav. 102
Constantia 113-4
containerization 17, 105, 112,
    114-7, 126-9
Cornwall, HMS 55
Crozier, HMS see *Protea*, HMSAS (1)
Cunard Line 54-6, 96, 165
Custodian **105**
da Gama, Vasco 8, 10
Dalia 111
Damaraland **120**
Dane (1) **100**
Danie du Plessis **40**, **167**
Danie Hugo **163**, **165**
Davis, Thomas B.F. 70
De Jonge Thomas **139**
Dean, Commodore F.J. 66
Delagoa Bay 8, 106, 140
Deutsch-Australische-
    Dampfschiffahrtges. 101
Deutsche-Afrika Linie 119
Deutsche Ost-Afrika Linie 20, 35,
    51, 77-9, 120
Devonshire, HMS **51**

Diaz, Bartholomew 8
Dominion Monarch 84
Doringbaai 173
Doris, HMS **23**
Dorsetshire, HMS 52, 55
Dover Castle (2) 83
D'Oyly Lyon, Vice-Admiral G.H. 58
Drake, Sir Francis 8
Drakenstein 113
Dreadnought, HMS (R.N.
    submarine) **61**
Dromedaris **4**
Duilio **35**, **92**
Dunbath **144**
Dunedin Star 144
Dunluce Castle 83
Dunottar Castle (1) 77
Dunvegan Castle (1) **26**
Durban Castle 84
Durban harbour 38-42, *et passim*
Durban Lines 123
Durham Castle 83
Dutch East India Company 10, 72,
    139, 171
E.S. Steytler **165**
Eagle, HMS **63**
East London harbour (*see also*
    Buffalo River) 34-7, 78, 87, 155
Eden, HMS see *Sonneblom*,
    HMSAS
Edinburgh Castle (2) 83
Edinburgh Castle (3) 14, **88**
Eduard Bohlen **142**
Eiken Maru **118**
Elder Dempster Lines 57
Elgaren (ro-ro vessel) **13**
Ellerman Lines (*see also* Ellerman
    and Bucknall) 119
Ellerman and Bucknall (*see also*
    Bucknall Brothers; Ellerman
    Lines) 26, 79, 90, 106-7, 119
Elphinstone, Vice-Admiral George
    Keith 47
Emden (2) **62**
Emily Hobhouse, SAS **69**
Empire Doon see *Pretoria*
Empire Fowey **132**
Empire Jewel see *Empire Fowey*
Empire Orwell see *Pretoria*
Empress of Britain 90
Empress of England **90**
Empreza Nacional de Nav. 102
Energy Endurance **125**
Enterprise 13
Erica (side trawler) **157**
Erica (SAR vessel) 111
Esmeralda **62**
Europa (1) (Italian liner) 92, **135**
Europa (2) (container vessel) 118
Evans, Vice-Admiral 61
Evgenia Chandris **137**
F. Schermbrucker **155**
F.C. Sturrock **165**
F.T. Bates **26**, **149**
Farrell Lines (*see also* Mallory
    Transport Lines) 26, 93, 108-9
Festivale see *S.A. Vaal*
fishing industry 156-7, 159
Flamingo, SAS (air-sea rescue
    base) 69
Flotta Lauro 135
Flying Dutchman **9**
Forresbank **107**
Fougstedt, Commodore H.E. 67
Foyle, HMS see *Immortelle*,
    HMSAS
France **96-7**
Franconia (1) 96
Franklin D. Roosevelt, USS **63**
Frean **144**
Galileo Galilei **135**
Galway Castle **141**
Gamtoos (1) **123**
Gamtoos (2) **4**, **123**
General Botha, SATS 70, **71**, 89, 100
General Botha (nautical academy) 71
General Screw Steam Ship
    Company 19, 100
George V, King of England 9
George M. Livanos **146**
Georgic **165**

Gertrud Woermann (1) **100**
Gertrud Woermann (2) **142**
Giulio Cesare 92
Gloria 63
Gneisenau (1) 51
Gondwana 125
Good Hope, HMS (R.N. cruiser) 51
Good Hope, SAS **65**
Good Hope Castle (2) **117**
Goorkha **26**
Gray, Vice-Admiral J.M.D. 61
Great Fish River 33
Green Point Common 49
Greta Delport 129
Grootekerk **107**
Grootvlei **157**
Grossherzogin Elizabeth **13**
Guglielmo Marconi **135**
H.T.V. Horner **167**
Hain Steam Ship Company 102
Hall, Lt. Commander D.A. 65
Hamburg Amerika Linie 101, 132
Hangklip 111
Hannoverland (1) 17
Hanka Sawicka **137**
Harrison Line 105-6, 119
Harry Escombe **163**
Hermes, HMS (R.N. cruiser) **47**
Highfields **140**
Holland-Afrika Lijn (*see also*
    Nedlloyd Line) 79, 91, 107, 127
Hong Kong Grace **147**
Hope 120
Horizon **150**
Howe, HMS **58**
Huntress **110**
Huntscliff see *Rufidji*
Ilderton **40**
Ile de France 54
Immortelle, HMSAS 64
Imperio 91
Infante Dom Henrique 91
Irvin and Johnson Ltd 157, 159
Italis see *America* (2)
Ixion **93**
J.D. White **165**
J.H. Botha **165**, **167**
J.R. More **162**, 165
Jagersfontein (1) **91**
Jagersfontein (2) 91, **127**
Jan van Riebeeck, SAS **67**
Johan Hugo 110, **111**
Johanna van der Merwe, SAS **69**
John Ross see *S.A. John Ross*
Johnson, Vice-Admiral J. **67**
Juan Sebastian de el Cano 62-3
Kaapland (1) **120**
Kaapland (2) **120**
Kadie **28**
Kaffir (Bucknall steamer) 106
Kaiser Wilhelm der Grosse 50
Karanja **90**
Karatara **121**
Karlsruhe **62**
Kazimah 149, **163**, 172
Kenilworth Castle (1) 83
Kenya Castle 84
Kimberley 82
Kinfauns Castle 51
Kiyo Maru 2 **152**
Klipfontein 91
Knysna 19, 28, 171
Königsberg 51
Kolsnaren (2) **128**
Kosmos IV **159**
Kowie **4**, **126**
Kronprinz 77
Kulu **125**
Kylsant Group (*see also* Bullard
    King) 103
Lake Manitoba **48**
Lambert's Bay 22-3, 49
Langkloof 113
LASH **126**
Lawhill **100**
Leach, Capt. J.C. 59
Letaba 113
Libertad 63
Liberty ships 107, 117
Llandovery Castle (1) 77
Llandovery Castle (2) 77

Llangibby Castle **83**
Llanstephan Castle **54-5**, 77
Lloyd, Commodore Norman 89
Lloyd Triestino 118-9, 135
Ludwig Wiener **82-3**, 162
Lüderitz 20, *et passim*
Lykes Lines 108
Mactra **146-7**, 172
Malgas 28
Mallory Transport Lines Inc. (*see also* Farrell Lines) 108
Manhattan see City of Lincoln (1)
Maori 141
Maputo *see* Delagoa Bay
Maria van Riebeeck, SAS 69
Mayflower X see Siroco-1
Medic 92
Mercury 169
Midway, USS 63
Mina 147
Mkuze **129**
Monarch, HMS **23**
Moore McCormack (*see also* United States Lines) 108, 127
Morgenster 113-4
Mormacaltair **127**
Mossel Bay 120
Mossel Bay 8, 29, 78, 169
Moçambique (2) 91
Nahoon (1) **121**
Namaqua *see Umzimvubu*
Namaqualand 120
Natal, SAS **65**
Natal Direct Line 72
Natal Naval Volunteers 64
Nedlloyd Kembla **118**
Nedlloyd Line (*see also* Holland-Afrika Lijn) 118
Neptune, HMS **58**, 77
Neptune Star see Erica
Nieuw Amsterdam 54
Nippon Yusen Kaisha 118
Njassa **35**
Nolloth **145**
Norddeutscher Lloyd 132
Norhval **159**
Northern Star 85, 93
Nyassa 77
Oceanic 168
Olympia 74
Oranjefontein 91
Oranjemund 23
Orcades (1) 54
Orient 141
Orient Line 54, 132, 134
Oriental Pioneer **152**
Orontes **132**
Orsova (2) **134**
Osaka Shosen Kaisha 118
Ostfriesland (1) 17
Oswego Guardian **147**
Otranto (2) 132
Ovambo 149
Overseas Container Lines 119
P. and O. Line 54, 58, 137
Pacific Steam Navigation Company 90
Pantelis A. Lemos 149
Patria 91
Pelagos **159**
Pendennis Castle 89
Penelope, HMS **23**
Perth, HMAS *see Amphion*, HMS
Phillips, Admiral Sir Tom 59
Pinguin 159
Popham, Admiral Sir Home Riggs 47
Port Alfred 19, 33
Port Beaufort 28, 121
Port Elizabeth harbour (*see also* Algoa Bay) 31, *et passim*
Port Frances *see* Port Alfred
Port Natal *see* Durban harbour
Port Nolloth 22, 50, 78, 100, 121, 126, 144
Port Shepstone 36-7
Port St Johns 19, 36-7, 40, 144
Portugal **102**
Portuguese Royal Mail Line 102
Potsdam (2) *see Empire Fowey*
Powerful, HMS **23**
President Kruger, SAS **67**

President Pretorius, SAS 67, **69**
President Steyn, SAS 67, **69**
Pretoria 78-9
Pretoria Castle (1) *see Warwick Castle* (4)
Pretoria Castle (2) (see also *S.A. Oranje*) 88-9
Prince of Wales, HMS **58-9**
Principe Perfeito 91
Produce 169
Protea, HMSAS (1) **28**, 64, **65**
Protea, HMSAS (2) 65
Protea, SAS (1) **66**
Protea, SAS (2) 65
Puma, HMS **61**
Python **52**
Queen Elizabeth 56, 96
Queen Elizabeth 2 96
Queen Mary 14, **55**, 56
Quelimane see Kronprinz
R.B. Waterston 165
Rambler, HM Survey Ship **23**
Randfontein (2) **91**
Range (1) **123**
Rei De Portugal 102
Reina del Mar 90
Rennies of Aberdeen 103, 105
Repulse, HMS 59
Rhodesia Castle 84
Richard's Bay 43, 126, 138, 155
Ridge **125**
Rio de Janeiro Maru 118
Robin Goodfellow 109
Robin Line 108-9
Rochester Castle **103**
Rockhampton Star **117**
Rockrose, HMS *see Protea*, SAS (1)
Romelia 152
ro-ro vessels'(*see also* containerization) 13, 126, 128
Roslin Castle (2) **73**
Roslin Castle (3) 103
Royal Rotterdam Lloyd 135
Royal Durban Light Infantry 54
Royal Interocean Lines 79, 91
Royal Mail Line 132
Royal Naval Volunteer Reserve (S.A.) 64
Royal Navy 13, 46, 50, 55, 58, 60, 67-9
RSA **168**
Rufidji 51
Runciman, John and William 74-5
Ruys 14, 79
S.A. Agulhas **168**, **170**
S.A. Alphen 115
S.A. Constantia 114
S.A. Helderberg 89, **115**
S.A. Hexrivier 113
S.A. John Ross 131, **168**
S.A. Langeberg **4**, **115**, 118
S.A. Merchant Naval Academy *see General Botha*, SATS
S.A. Morgenster 26
S.A. Oranje (see also *Pretoria Castle* (2)) 14, **19**, 87, **88-9**, 163
S.A. Oranjeland 141, **149**
S.A. Seafarer **150-1**
S.A. Sederberg 115
S.A. Shipowners' Association 70
S.A. Vaal (1) 43, 85, **87**, **89**
S.A. Vaal (2) 116
S.A. van der Stel 114
S.A. Vergelegen **17**, 114
S.A. Winterberg **42**
S.A. Wolraad Woltemade 131, **168**
S.A. Zebediela 113
Safari Service 116
Safina-E-Hujjaj see Empire Fowey
Safmarine 16-7, 112-8, *et passim*
Sagafjord **96**
Saldanha, Battle of 47
Saldanha Bay 22-3, 54, 69, 126, 129, 146, 173
San Jerome 138
Santos Maru 118
São João 37
Scharnhorst (1) 51
Schulschiff Deutschland **62**
Scot 14, **76-7**
Seattle 110

Seaward Defence Force 64
Seawise University see Queen Elizabeth
Shaw Savill and Albion Co. 78-9, 84, 92, 141
ship repair industry 17, 172-3
shipbuilding industry 171
shipwrecks (*see also* names of specific ships) 138-53
Sierra Pedrosa see Brutus
Simferopol 146
Simon van der Stel, SAS 67
Simon's Bay (*see also* Simonstown harbour) 23, 47, 50, 64
Simonstown Agreement 68-9
Simonstown harbour (*see also* Simon's Bay) 23, 50-1, 55-6, 60-1, 67-8, 103
Sinde 125
Sir Charles Elliott 144
Sir David Hunter 103
Sir Robert Peel 19, 121
Sir William Hoy 165
Siroco-1 **152**
Sishen (*see also* Saldanha Bay) 22, 129
Sishen 117
Skeleton Coast 144, 146
Slangkop lighthouse 149
Smith's Coasters 121, 123
Somtseu 37
Sonneblom, HMSAS 64, **65**
South Africa **101**
South African Lines 120
South African Marine Corporation *see* Safmarine
South African Merchant **112**, **113**
South African merchant navy 16
South African Naval Forces 55, 64
South African Naval Service 64
South African Navy 13, 44, 46, 60-1, 65-9
South African Victory **113**
South Atlantic Station 50-1, 60, 85
Southampton, HMS 46
Southampton Castle **117**
Southern Africa/Europe Container Service 119
Southern Barrier, HMSAS **65**
Southern Cross **92-3**
Southern Maid, HMSAS 65
Springbok Shipping Company 112
St George, HMS **47**
St Helena 94-5
States Marine Corporation 112
Stella Polaris 78
Stellenberg 152
Stirling Castle (2) 14, 76, 82, 85
Storms River mouth 29
strike craft, Minister-class **44**, **69**
Suez Canal 130-2, 137, 172
Sugela 116
Suiderkruis 161
Sussex, HMS 52
Swakopmund 20, 77, 100
Swale, HMS **52**
Swazi **22**
Sybille, HMS 49
T. Eriksen 167
T.H. Watermeyer 149, **163**, 165
T.S. McEwen **26**, 146, 149, **163**
Table Bay (SAL vessel) 120
Table Bay (container vessel) 119
Table Bay (*see also* Table Bay harbour) 8-9, *et passim*
Table Bay harbour 24-6, *et passim*
Tafelberg (factory ship) **159**
Tafelberg, SAS 67, **69**
Tegelberg 14, 79
Testbank 78
Texaco North America 125
Texanita 147
Thames, HMS *see General Botha*, SATS
Theodore Woker see E.S. Steytler
Thermopylae 140
Thesens Steamship Company 28, 123, 144
Thomas T. Tucker 145
Thomson, Commodore Robin 89
Thor (German raider) 56, 85, 159

Thorshope **119**
Thrush, HMS **23**
Tina Onassis **125**
Tjisadane **91**
Tottenham, Vice-Admiral 61
Transvaal, SAS 65
Transvaal (4) **119**
Transvaal Castle (see also *S.A. Vaal*) 85, 89
Trewidden **102**
Tung, C.Y. 56, 125, 147
Tzaneen 113
U-27 47
U-172 54
U-178 59
U-182 111
U-714 65
Umfolozi **123**
Umgeni (1) **49**
Umgeni (3) **57**
Umhlali 149
Umtali (2) **57**
Umtata (2) **49**
Umtata (3) 57
Umvoti (2) **103**
Umzimvubu 144
Uni-2 **161**
Unicorn Lines 123, *et passim*
Union-Castle Line 76-7, 80-9, 103, 117, *et passim*
Union Line (*see also* Union-Castle Line) 77, 100
Union Steam Ship Company *see* Union Line
United States **97**
United States Lines (*see also* Moore McCormack) 108, 136
United States Shipping Board 108
Uruguay Star 135

Valdivia 141
van der Stel, Simon 34
van Riebeeck, Jan 4, 138
Vanguard, HMS **61**
Velma Lykes 109
Vergelegen 89, 113-4
Victorious, HMS (aircraft carrier) **63**
Victory **117**
Victory ships 107, 112-3
Vistafjord **31**, 96
Voortrekker (1) **121**
Voortrekker (rig tender) **169**
W.H. Andrag **167**
Wafra 168
Waimerama 77
Wakasa Maru 118
Walvis Bay 20, 50, 59, 78, 155
Walvis Bay 120
Wanderer 105
Wangoni 20
Waratah 40, **142**
Warrior, HMS (aircraft carrier) 63
Warwick Castle (3) 82
Warwick Castle (4) **84**
Watussi 52
Weserland (1) 17
Wessex, HMS *see Jan van Riebeeck*, SAS
West Point see Australis
whaling industry 159-61
Whelp, HMS *see Simon van der Stel*, SAS
White Star Line 78, 92
Willem Barendsz **160**
Willem Heckroodt 167
Willem Ruys see Achille Lauro
Winchester Castle **82**
Windhuk **78-9**
Windsor Castle (1) 148
Windsor Castle (2) 81
Windsor Castle (3) **4**, 14, **26**, **73**, 82, 89
Woermann Linie 100, 142
Wolf 50
Wolraad Woltemade see S.A. Wolraad Woltemade
Woltemade, Wolraad 139
World War, First 50-1, *et passim*
World War, Second 52-9, *et passim*
Ysterfontein 160
Zulu 149
Zwartkops 129